Small Antiques for the Small Home

Small Antiques
for the Small Home

Sheila Stuart

South Brunswick • New York: A.S. Barnes and Company
London: Thomas Yoseloff Ltd

A. S. Barnes and Co., Inc.
Cranbury, New Jersey 08512

Thomas Yoseloff Ltd
18 Charing Cross Road
London W.C. 2, England

6757
Printed in the United States of America

For Effie
with my love.

Contents

Small Antiques for the Small Home

1

The Delight of the Mirror

There is something endearing about the small antique which is denied to the larger pieces of furniture. A beautiful pedestal dining table, a finely proportioned four poster bed, a tall bureau bookcase — all these may be charming but they need a spacious background and must be carefully placed. Even then, one does not love them as one loves the little chair, the tiny stool, the small wall mirror, the sampler and the host of little things one collects for a small home.

Mirrors are among the more modern of antiques. It was not until the sixteenth century that glass mirrors were known in England to any great extent. They are not mentioned in the Inventories of the first Elizabeth but as travellers to Italy — and notably to Venice, the important center of glass making on the Continent — began to bring specimens home as gifts it seems not unlikely that there would be several examples of mirrored glass in the royal palaces.

But they were scarce and Elizabeth performed her toilette with the aid of burnished metals such as brass, copper, steel or silver which were used also by the grandees at Court. However, the art of making glass mirrors had been practiced for centuries by the Egyptians, though it remained a secret until the Crusaders brought the knowledge from Egypt to Venice.

But just as the Egyptians had been unwilling to pass on their skills so were the Venetians jealous of sharing their acquired knowledge and kept it closely to themselves. So while glass factories were set up in Italy and a thriving business was built up in the manufacture of mirrors which were widely sold throughout Europe, the actual mirrors were exported but not the manner of making them.

Consequently when small mirrors began to appear in England from the time of Henry VIII onwards, these were imported, usually from Venice. It is surprising that the secret of making looking glasses was so slow in reaching England, for glass works had been in existence at Chiddingford, in Surrey, as early as the fourteenth century. During the progressive reign of Elizabeth foreigners began to obtain patents for the manufacture of "glass panes" and drinking vessels.

Scotland was ahead of England in the industry, as mirrors had been introduced there during the reign of James V, father of Mary Queen of Scots, by the Flemings who as early as the late fourteenth century had been renowned on the Continent as glass makers, and their names appeared in an Inventory of Charles V of France (Charles the Wise) who died in 1380. To a limited extent glass mirrors had been produced in Scotland in the sixteenth century and were mentioned in the Royal Scottish Inventories of 1578.

Sir Robert Mansel or Mansell was one of the Scottish pioneers in making mirrored glass, and in 1615 James VI — first of England — granted him a permit for the manufacture of "looking glass plates." Three years later he received a monopoly for the "sole making of glasses." So successful was his venture that several hundred workmen are reputed to have been employed in his Scottish factory. He was aided also by some exiled Venetians — including one Leonardo Michellini — who passed on their knowledge to the Scots.

It was not for another forty years or so, at the time of the Restoration on the return of Charles II from exile in France, that the factory at Vauxhall was set up by the Duke of Buckingham for the manufacture of glass and mirrored plates. This was really the beginning of what was to prove a most successful industry.

The number of mirrors reaching England from Europe, and from Venice in particular, was hastened by two factors. One was the increasing interest in foreign travel which had been fostered by the Elizabethans and which since then had continued to grow. It became modish to take the grand European tour which invariably included Italy, and nobles brought back with them examples of real looking glasses to charm their womenfolk at home. The other factor was the custom of those days for monarchs to make valuable gifts to each other, and what could be more highly prized than the presentation of a real Venetian mirror?

But glass mirrors were costly and the metal looking glass continued to be used in England by those who could not afford real mirrored glass. After the death of Charles I several glass mirrors were among the king's effects. One presumably had belonged to Cardinal Wolsey for it was described as having "Cardinal arms on ye topp."

It was probably Charles II who brought the authentic mirror within reasonable reach of the English. During his exile Charles had learned much of the finer things of life, and on his return from France he proceeded to translate many of his new ideas into the general background of his own country. Many of these were expressed in house interiors, in elegant hangings, and in finer furniture than had been hitherto known; and appointments began to appear in the homes of the upper classes which they had not known before. In a word Charles translated culture into an enviable and delightful possession. It might be said he was the first cultured king of England.

Evelyn, the celebrated diarist of the seventeenth century, summed it up neatly when he said, "he brought a politer way of living." It was perhaps fortunate that England was ready for an aesthetic improvement in her social way of life, and novelties brought about by Charles "matched the hour." In addition to popularizing the arts one of his most striking innovations was the impetus he gave to the manufacture of mirrored glass, and by his keen interest in it from a commercial angle.

A good deal of this was a direct result of French influence, for many Venetian workmen had broken away from the Italian glass houses and had set up factories in France and in the Low Countries. It was largely due to this that he gave such encouragement to his friend George Villiers to start glass making at Vauxhall.

Charles' artistic tendencies came to England after a barren period for during the protectorate of Cromwell the making of mirrors was not looked on with favor, possibly because it seemed to savor too much of frivolity and vanity, and was not produced in any real numbers until the Restoration.

A magnificent mirror is said to have been presented to Francis I of France by the then ambassador from Venice. He was born in 1494 and died in 1547, and was therefore a contemporary of Henry VIII of England, and so he possessed this piece which was the height of luxury and opulence but about a hundred and thirty years before the glass works were erected at Vauxhall.

It was quickly recognized that the looking glass plates made at Vauxhall were vastly superior in quality to any that had already been produced in England. Indeed Evelyn wrote in his diary after a visit to the glass works that he saw "glasses far larger and better than any that came from Venice." English craftsmen learned so well from the foreigners that their products were more than equal to those of Venice. This was admitted and also that the Vauxhall mirrors gave a truer reflection than any type of mirror plate hitherto known.

Considering the extreme fragility of glass and that it was in such frequent use it is astonishing that in so many antique mirrors the original glass still exists. This is highly rated but it is not always an asset. The presence of the old glass creates a problem because in many cases the glass is not only tarnished but it gives a distorted reflection, especially in the larger plates; most possessors of old mirrors have to face at one time or another the decision, whether to retain the mirror as it is — even though it may not present a true reflection — or do away with a glass which is no longer a mirror in the real sense of the word, and replace it with a modern sheet of glass.

Some collectors follow the school of thought which considers that an old piece should never be altered, and they prefer to retain the original glass simply because it is old, but where a mirror is placed as an aid to performing one's toilette it seems a doubtful point to keep it when it is no longer able to fulfill the function for which it was made. A connoisseur may not hesitate about indulging his love for the old at the expense of convenience but anyone who has tried to dress with the aid of a much spotted glass which however valuable gives a misleading impression might revise his opinion on the subject.

At the same time the charm of old glass should not be overlooked. Because of the extreme thinness of the glass used it has a greater depth of reflection as well as a dark, almost mysterious quality which makes it easy to identify. The edges of Vauxhall glass are bevelled but the bevelling is so slight that it can scarcely be felt by the hand. Where it is reasonably well preserved the existence of the old glass in a mirror increases its value.

At first, glass mirrors were small because the early glass workers had not the skill and knowledge to make the larger mirror plates, and large mirrors in one piece were not produced until the middle years of the eighteenth century. Where an extensive looking glass was essential, small pieces of mirrored glass were joined together as in an overmantel over a chimney piece, in order to give the effect of a large mirror.

The very early English mirrors dating from the first half of the seventeenth century were all small. Those were the first real mirrors known to the Englishwoman of the period and were the ancestors of all dressing table looking glasses. They were made after the style of a photo frame and by means of a hinged strut were able to stand on a dressing table. Hence their name — strut glasses.

Those little pioneers of the dressing table were delightful extravagancies, essentially feminine, and great stress was laid on the frames which were of the finest materials — embossed silver or gilt, galloon, marqueterie, or tortoiseshell. Because of their size they could be conveniently packed when their owners left home on the long visits to friends which were undertaken by the upper classes in those days.

Gradually it became fashionable for a woman of quality to own a small toilet glass and new ideas for frames which would enrich the glass were constantly being introduced. Wooden frames were poppular, such as olive and laburnum and were often square in shape. One of the most lavish types was a silver frame richly embossed, and in the case of a noble or Court official it was ornamenated with a coronet and cypher.

Veneer and marquetry are typical of those times and must have added considerable elegance to fashionable bedrooms. Those with a plain walnut veneer, with the walnut cut at right angles to the molding, are attractive but specimens are rare. In the Inventory of Charles I, there is mention of mirrors framed in ebony and inlaid with mother of pearl, while others enumerated are of needlework.

Belonging to the same period are marquetry frames worked out in a floral design sometimes with the addition of a bird in natural woods such as rosewood, ebony and cherry. An alternative pattern is the seaweed design but these are less plentiful, as by the time it was introduced marquetry was losing its appeal.

When those early frames were made they were looked on as being of greater importance and more valuable than the actual mirror which they surrounded, and this may explain why some of the old mirrored glass was thrown out and the mirrors retained. The strut type of looking glass is rarely seen nowadays save in a museum or private collection. It is agreeable to discover, however, that many other old mirrors of a slightly later period are still to be found and among the most charming and decorative of these is the wall mirror.

Here it may be said that while it is often taken for granted that the first mirrors of this kind were of glass, this is not so, as there are records of little hanging mirrors made of burnished gold, silver and bronze, these having been used by the nobility as early as the fifteenth century.

It was in the first half of the seventeenth century, circa 1639, that hanging mirrors began to be used in the London homes of the great, and they were also found in country houses in the more remote areas. All this gave work to the Vauxhall glass factory, but in addition to producing mirrored glass Vauxhall had another speciality — that of making plate glass which was used for the glass put into coaches.

Encouraged by the success of Vauxhall, other skilled workers began to set up more ambitious glass works, and in the last decade of the seventeenth century it was said by a Mr. Gumley, who with his partners had built a new glass house, "that the trade of Looking Glass Plates is so considerably improved that they serve not only for furniture and ornament in her Majesty's Dominions at home, but are likewise in great esteem in foreign parts; the Venetians themselves buying these plates and preferring them before their own."

"It is likewise evident that since Mr. Gumley's undertaking Looking Glass Plates are made larger and better, and the price of them fallen . . . which is not only a benefit to he Majesty's subjects, but a great encouragement to Exportation."

John Gumley had other interests for he was also a cabinet maker in the time of Queen Anne and of George I, and there are records that in the early years of the eighteenth century he became cabinet maker to the Crown and supplied both furniture and looking glasses to the nobility of England of that day. His workshop was in the New Exchange in the Strand and he called it his "glass gallery." So attractive were his goods that it became a fashionable place of resort. It was pulled down in 1737.

From the time of Queen Anne onwards the making of mirrors was a flourishng industry fast increasing, and a lively export market was extending to an equally great extent. According to R. W. Symonds "the making of an export trade of look-ing glasses, of the yearly value at that time, of fifty thousand pounds, shows to what degree the English craftsmen had excelled in the making of this particular produce during a short space."

But it was with the advent of the eighteenth century that mirrors really came into their own. The early seventeen hundreds saw a great surge of blossoming in social customs and particularly in the furnishing habits of the nobility and of the new middle classes. It was a graceful time for the debut of the mirror.

Charles II had brought the looking glass as a startling luxury for the fortunate few but its success had been so phenomenal that it was fast becoming an elegant asset of every day life, not only for the Court beauties but for women much further down the social scale. It seems peculiarly appropriate that there should have blossomed in the enchanting times of Queen Anne this feminine delight, which was to be of such value not only to the lovelies of the day but to all women who were to come after them.

The arrival of the mirror symbolized the change that was invading all English ideas in furniture and furnishing. Until the end of the seventeenth century, furniture had been heavy and large, and even in the homes of the wealthy it was limited, not only in design but in the number of pieces in actual use. Commercial enterprise in the Far East had brought a new prosperity to the country which in turn helped to create a fresh section of society. This was the new Middle Class who spent lavishly on luxuries and viewed the old methods through unconventional eyes. It was as if everything were changing at once. Furnishing took on a new importance and the wealthy suddenly awoke to the excitement of good taste.

With the accession of William and Mary there came a vogue for gilt wall mirrors which were less heavy than of yore and sometimes showed the owner's crest and coronet. The growing good taste was immediately reflected in the designs for the Queen Anne mirrors. The rather squat, square shape of the Carolean looking glass gave way overnight, almost, to the longish hanging mirror arched at the top and supremely decorative.

Frames were now much narrower. Glass, both cut and engraved, continued to be used for frames but very soon carved wood and gilt cresting replaced the glass and this was succeeded by the familiar frames of walnut. Mirrors with glass borders were out but they were popular again later in the century, about 1760. It was the early walnut mirror with its very pleasing lines which laid the foundation of the almost perfect mirror designs which prevailed throughout the century.

Walnut had supplanted oak as the fashionable wood and a characteristic Queen Anne mirror has a narrow perpendicular frame of walnut, with flattened sides and a shaped arched top. A typical touch is a narrow fillet of gilt fitted between the glass and the frame — an inspired touch of elegance which persisted throughout the century on frames of mahogany as well as of walnut.

While this design is the essence of simplicity it has a charm which later examples, some of them elaborate, failed to achieve. Though it lacked carving and ornament and had no superfluity of line its design has never been improved upon and indeed it has been copied by modern manufacturers.

So long as craftsmen were unable to make large plates of mirrored glass, mirrors continued to be small but the desire for a larger looking glass was so pronounced that glass workers produced one by joining several pieces of glass together. Hanging mirrors showed a join about a third of the way down and when the horizontal mirror placed across the chimney piece was in vogue, this could only be done by joining the requisite number of small plates together. While those joined mirrors were so made from necessity the effect was strikingly effective, so much so that the "joined glasses" continued in use long after mirrors were produced in one piece.

Later in the century designs appeared which were less restrained. Escallop shells were carved in the edges of the framing and cresting and other types of ornamentation were expressed in fine carving and gilt gesso. As workers grew more skilled in cutting, oval and circular mirrors were made, and these were greatly in demand, but the extreme amount of cutting, which was necessary for those shapes, resulted in a loss to the manufacturer and the cost was prohibitive.

Though they are by no means plentiful it is not impossible to come upon examples of those early

Joined eighteenth-century glass. May be hung or placed above the chimney piece. (Courtesy John Bell)

mirrors including those of joined glass. Sometimes the surface of the glass on overmantels was painted with various scrolls such as a star, a cypher or a coronet. Robert Adam was one of the craftsmen who liked this form of decoration and he used it a lot, and the result lent an increased sparkle of gaiety to the fashionable assemblies of the eighteenth century. This was enhanced by the reflection thrown back from the chimney piece mirror and also by the glittering wall mirrors by which the drawing rooms of that era were decorated.

At one period the vogue for looking glasses had reached such a pitch that among the wealthier classes they were employed so lavishly as to outstrip good taste in many cases. It is said that in the seventeenth century, Nell Gwynne had one of the rooms in her house hung entirely with mirrors — the forerunner perhaps of some of the modern restaurant modes.

Inevitably as the workers learned how to make large glass plates the joined mirrors disappeared. With the advent of the large looking glasses the frames which had been of such consequence earlier in the century now became of secondary interest to the actual glass. It was about the middle of the eighteenth century that the carved gilt frame for the hanging mirror appeared, and as the Queen

Anne mirrors had been revolutionary in their time, so once again this fresh advance struck a new note.

Of narrow gilt, finely carved or even twisted into an open pattern giving a delightful delicate effect, this was indeed a successful fashion touch. Sometimes the mirror was oval shaped and had a rococo style of decoration cresting the top and this also was new. Sometimes there was a shell ornament at the bottom and this gave a finish of elegance.

Perhaps the most popular were those with the open carving. They were usually perpendicular in shape though occasionally there was a reversion to the older square style. Chippendale made many of those open carved wall mirrors and though they were out of fashion for many years and were sometimes discarded as being of no consequence, they have again staged a comeback and are in great demand though they are not too numerous.

The wall looking glass had its greatest triumph when Chippendale produced one which was not only different from those others which had preceded it, but had so many attributes desirable in a mirror, that it was known then and has been known since as a Chippendale mirror. It was a novelty in that while Chippendale did not entirely

Typical Chippendale mahogany mirror. Very fine fretwork and gilt eagle inset in aperture at top. (Courtesy John Bell)

neglect walnut, which had been the popular wood for the smaller pieces since the early years of the century, for this frame he used mahogany.

This change of wood lent additional scope for treatment and decoration and its success resulted in a wall mirror whose beauty of design has never been improved. Other craftsmen of the time also made mirrors of considerable charm but none of them surpassed those turned out by Chippendale and the workmen who labored under his supervision.

Those wall mirrors must have been made in great numbers for they are still comparatively plentiful. They differ in size and in detail but the overall design is common to them all. They hang perpendicularly and the best known design is the familiar fretted mahogany frame with a broken pediment at the top and sometimes, but not always, there is a crested eagle. Occasionally another touch may be a tiny finial filling the space in the center of the pediment.

Early Chippendale wall mirror with fretwork top and bottom. Gilt inset between mirror and frame. (Courtesy John Bell)

Chippendale gilt mirror, beautifully shaped and richly carved. Branched candlesticks at base. (Courtesy John Bell)

The sides of the frame are reeded and the bottom is fretted, and almost invariably a narrow gilt fillet divides the frame from the actual glass. Some specimens have a branched candlestick fitted at the base of the mirror thus giving the impression of added light.

As Chippendale designed and made furniture for the owners of large mansions, and indeed specialized in this, many of his mirrors were intended for spacious drawing rooms and were about three or four feet in height, while others for smaller rooms were barely a foot high. All of them were charming, and all, once one has been introduced to this Chippendale mirror, are readily identifiable.

The Chippendale mirror is most easily placed, blending happily not only among pieces of approximately its own period, but looking equally at home against a modern background. The very small Chippendale wall glass is a delectable piece and is worth looking for. It differs from the larger examples in that it does not always have a gilt fillet and the sides and bottom may be quite plain.

In the little mirror the only decoration is the restrained fretting along the top of the frame. This has no broken pediment but is quite straight, and there is often no fret at the base. Chippendale mirrors both large and small very frequently still have the original glass and this gives forth a dark fascinating reflection, absent in modern mirrors.

Collectors who are still at the early stages in looking out for desirable pieces should note that mention of any piece of furniture to which the name of Chippendale is attached does not imply that he was necessarily personally concerned with its production. Chippendale conceived the designs and many were indeed made in his workshops, and in his cabinet maker's establishment, but he also produced a book of his designs and those were sold throughout the country. Also, they were copied by other skilled craftsmen and were sold as Chippendale. The same applies to the work of the other eminent cabinet makes of the day — Hepplewhite, Adam and Sheraton.

A more striking innovation than the wall mirror was the introduction, during the reign of Queen Anne, of the small toilet swing glass. To appreciate the importance of this invention, for it really was an invention, one has to remember that until the beginning of the eighteenth century there had not been a mirror specifically intended for a woman's toilette, and as a successor to the strut glass it must have created a minor sensation in the fashionable bedrooms of the time.

It was the advent of the toilet mirror which hastened the arrival of the dressing table, for while females of earlier days must have demanded a table on which to lay the appurtenances of the toilet — brushes, combs, powders, pencils and perfume — the table was simply a casual piece of furniture not designed for that purpose.

History has repeated itself in that there is not always sufficient space in a small modern bedroom for an adequate dressing table, and in a guest room particularly the small rectangular table, fitted perhaps with a couple of drawers, often performs the same function as it did in the pre-dressing-table days.

Early swing glasses were framed in walnut, the wood of the period. The looking glass was made to pivot between turned or square supports and

Delightful carved Chippendale mirror of the mid-eighteenth century. Of richly carved pine gilt wood in a handsome design. (Courtesy Charles Lumb)

rested on a box base fitted with a horizontal row of tiny drawers, or sometimes a double row after the manner of a tiny bureau which was very typical of the Queen Anne toilet glass. The most desirable types were made with a serpentine front which was most elegant. The little drawers merit notice as they were dove-tailed and beautifully made, and had small ivory knobs for handles.

Influenced by the high fashion styles frames were perpendicular and reached up to mirror the piled-up hair. The upper part tapered slightly with a side cresting reminiscent of the wall mirrors, and was arched at the top. Again, too, a fillet of gilt was inset between the glass and the frame. Sometimes lacquer was used as a finish on the walnut and one such glass was ordered for Queen Anne circa 1704, described as having "a dressing glass on a swinging frame, Japan'd with an arched top."

Pleasing though it was, this type of swing glass had quite a short life and by the time George I succeeded Anne in 1714, not only was there a change in design but a change as well in the wood employed. Mahogany by then was becoming the popular wood and was partly ousting walnut. Some

An unusually plain Chippendale mirror in mahogany. Rectangular glass reeded at sides and top and bottom. Small box base with three drawers. (Courtesy John Bell)

Early walnut hanging mirror with gilt inset. Fret at top and candlestick at base. (Courtesy John Bell)

Very early strut glass to be used on a dressing table. (Courtesy John Bell)

High walnut Queen Anne mirror with arched top. Turned supports and deep base with double row of drawers. (Courtesy John Bell)

Very rare old Queen Anne mirror of walnut with shaped glass, solid supports, and deep box base. (Courtesy John Bell)

Dainty Hepplewhite serpentine dressing glass, with oval mirror and shaped supports. Inlay on drawers and resting on small bracket feet. (Courtesy John Bell)

walnut glasses still persisted, however, but showed the newer trend by being cross banded in the new wood.

Georgian toilet mirrors no longer had a double tier of drawers but were fitted with a single row of three drawers horizontally placed, and were either straight fronted or bow fronted, or were finished with a modified but elegant serpentine shaping. This base rested on small bracket feet.

By the middle years of the century oval and circular mirrors were in favor and the side supports were curved to follow the line of the glass. This type was used a good deal by Hepplewhite. Ivory knobs or tiny brass rings were used as handles and the center drawer was usually fitted with a small ivory keyhole. This type of swing glass was made by all the famous cabinet makers of the day and its modest proportions and clean-cut lines make it an ideal piece to look for.

About the end of the century Sheraton brought back the double-box type which he finished with a curved base resting on little bun feet. In this design the top layer of drawers was slightly recessed and while it was attractive enough, it lacked the appeal of the earlier examples.

Towards the end of the eighteenth century when hair was again worn high on the head the shorter type of looking glass did not give a complete reflection, and the longer perpendicular mirror was once more fashionable. Sheraton decorated such glasses with cross banding in satinwood an ornamentation which was very popular.

About this time the box base gradually became less important until in some specimens it was omitted altogether. It was replaced by a stretcher, shaped or curved or even straight and this, though it looked slender, was sufficient to keep the uprights in position. These rested on yoke feet. The drawers which had been on all the toilet glasses since the time of Queen Anne were very often absent. The glass was called a skeleton glass.

By the turn of the century designs again underwent a change because of another change in hairdressing modes. The high towering coiffure was out of date, having given way to the classical style whereby the hair was brushed flat and close to the sides of the head, and as the tall mirror was no longer essential it was replaced by a rectangular

Graceful Hepplewhite dressing glass with oval mirror. Three small drawers. Made of mahogany and cross banded in tulip wood. (Courtesy John Bell)

Eighteenth-century skeleton mahogany dressing glass. Oval-shaped mirror on curved supports. (Courtesy John Bell)

shape. But the long run of good taste was drawing to an end and the glasses of that era were no exception losing much of their original elegance.

The skeleton glass usually had turned supports and a turned stretcher between the yoked feet and on some examples the frame was relieved by cross banding and dainty, vase-shaped finials — a design which is still in modified demand and is not so hard to come by as some of the earlier swing glasses.

The early nineteenth century brought about a further debasement in styles. Circa the second decade a new kind of box base appeared. It was rather bulky with two horizontal drawers set in with a front shaped like the side of a bible. But there was an ungainly gap between the frame and the box base which made the general effect clumsy, so that today it is among the least desirable of the small toilet mirrors.

A chapter on mirrors suitable for the modern home should have a reference to the small circular wall mirrors which were produced about the turn of the eighteenth century. These are the convex and the concave mirrors and they do not give true reflections. The convex presents a diminishing effect and the concave magnifies it, so that in that sense they are not so much looking glasses as wall decorations. These small mirrors have a broad gilt frame usually carved and frequently crested with an eagle. In appearance they are astonishingly modern. Of the two the concave is the more popular.

Then there is the cheval glass. In this connection the word cheval means "large" because when they were first introduced by Sheraton towards the end of the eighteenth century a big mirror was still unusual because all workers had not yet learned how to make large plates of glass. Authorities differ as to when it first appeared, but 1785 seems a likely date for the arrival of the charming and to us essential bedroom mirror.

And yet the early chevals must be among the few pieces made in the eighteenth century for which there is little demand nowadays. They were probably made in outside proportions because a really large mirror was an achievement at the time. But there was nothing graceful about this somewhat unwieldy mirror and the chevals most popular today are copies made in a much more slender edition.

Circular convex mirror with gilt frame, surmounted by an eagle. Candlesticks at base. (Courtesy John Bell)

The cheval mirror was built on the same lines as the little toilet glass. It was swung between supports with turned finials, and the supports rested on legs which were shaped and curved and mounted on casters for convenience when the cheval had to be moved from one place to another in the room.

Near the top of the side supports little candelabra or branching candlesticks were fixed to give additional light during the making of the toilet, and sometimes at the sides litle fitments of tiny drawers were attached to contain the toilet requisites. As in the case of the small toilet mirror the cheval could be tilted back and forth as required, while the mirror proper was made so that it could also be raised or lowered by means of a screw, so as to accommodate the reflection of the user.

Made with the usual skill of the eighteenth century cabinet makers the cheval was more estimable than beautiful but nobody could deny its usefulness and when it was first produced it must have been in terrific demand. It possessed so many good points that it was unfortunate that it should have lacked what was considered one of the most appealing factors of the time — grace.

It was not until the nineteenth century was well advanced that the design was altered to make it a slender and virtually a new piece.

2

Table Glass

Included among the attractive little pieces which can be carried home in the pocket or in the handbag are the small dram or cordial glasses. They are lovely to look at and in addition to their own intrinsic beauty it is no problem to place them where they can best catch the light. A dining table is one of the most satisfactory backgrounds for them, especially at night where an overhead bulb will make a picture out of every glass.

Those small dram glasses were typical in most homes during the latter half of the seventeenth century and perhaps even more so throughout the convivial times of the eighteenth. Drinks of considerable potency were the mainstay of seventeenth century assemblies and parties, and were symbolic of the domestic revelry of the day. One of the recipes consisted of 50 per cent alchohol, 25 per cent sugar, with fruit juices and essence of herbs making up the last 25 per cent.

If guests were to remain in a state of sobriety it is understandable that the mixture would have to be taken in small quantities only if undiluted. In recognition of this, cordial glasses of limited capacity were produced for the home consumption of the fashionable world, but larger types presumably intended for more extravagant tippling were the accepted thing at more extensive gatherings.

Wine glasses, *c.* 1815, with bell-shaped bowls and circular bases. (Courtesy John Bell)

A glass of cordial was known at first as a dram cup but this was later changed to a dram glass. About the end of the seventeenth century the cordial glass tended to follow a distinct pattern

23

Unusually fine English glass, *c.* 1765. Cutting on stem
and on base, and engraved trading scene on bowl.
(Courtesy Arthur Churchill)

with a heavy bucket shaped bowl and a thick
solid base. A writer is on record as having said
in 1663, "Fetch me the cordial glass in the Cabinet
window," presumably the first published mention
of this piece.

The cordial as a drink was introduced into
English society about the time of the Restoration
and "dramming" was associated particularly with
such spirits as whisky, gin, brandy and rum and
"to take a dram" implied knocking back those
drinks at one go. This expression is still used in
Scotland when a drink is offered and also, though

to a lesser degree, in England. In a letter dated
1682 John Bunyan used the word "dram" when
he said "I have a cordial the which, sir, if you
will take a dram of, may make you bonnie and
blithe."

When dram glasses first appeared they were designed like small tumblers very tiny indeed, less
than two inches in height, and this limited capacity is some indication of the strength of the tipple
likely to be drunk. In the early designs the tumbler
rested on four little feet, and as English glass
making at that time was still very much under the

Attractive wine glass with four knopped stems and spiral bands. *c. 1770* (Courtesy John Bell)

the result that the glass trade between Italy and England increased tremendously. It should be remembered that the glass trade in England was in its infancy at that time and the home production just beginning. But in spite of the many drinking glasses which were then imported, very few of the survivals have been identified as "Greene" glasses. This is the more remarkable when one remembers how precious such glasses must have been and one would imagine that in spite of their fragility they would have been carefully preserved.

Wine glass with a round funnel bowl engraved with a courting scene. Beautifully cut stem. *c. 1785.* (Courtesy Arthur Churchill)

influence of Venetian styles, they were decorated with two rows of prunts or raised "icicles" in the traditional Italian manner.

But drinking glasses were in a transitional period just then, and Englishmen were begining to discover that the Venetian designs were not necessarily suited to their own special needs or their brand of drink. It fell to one John Greene, a dealer both in drinking glasses and in looking glasses, to try to supply the needs of his countrymen in this respect.

To obtain the kind of glasses which he believed would please his customers, Greene, who had a certain skill in drawing, hit on the idea of making drawings of various glasses which appealed to him, and sending them to be copied by the workmen in Venice. This was most successful and from about 1667 large numbers of glasses ordered by Greene from Italy were imported into England over a number of years.

Other English merchants copied his ideas with

As well as the very small tumblers made by Greene, he also produced others in different sizes, large ones for wine and beer and smaller ones for brandy. The design was plain, or else ribbed horizontally or perpendicularly, and sometimes they were adorned with surface molding.

An unusual feature for the times was the arrangement of tumblers of different sizes, in "nests" containing as many as ten or twelve glasses. While tumblers were known in the reign of Queen Anne, early examples are rare, though they were made in their present shape from about 1715. Some were engraved with sprays of roses, others with hops and barley and are slightly tapered.

The early small shapes are more attractive than the later specimens of the early nineteenth century, which are squat and heavy and, though sometimes tall, are lavishly cut. Tumblers of themselves have never held much appeal and their charm lies chiefly in the cuting where this is found. As the design has varied so little they are not easy to date.

It is worth mentioning that while much prominence has been given to the glass works set up at Vauxhall at the time of the Restoration, it is not generally known that Elizabeth had also lent her patronage to the making of glass in England about a century earlier. In 1575 an Italian worker from Venice, Jacopo Verzelini, set up his furness at Crutched Friars, and received from the queen a patent for 21 years enabling him to manufacture drinking glasses of the type he had been accustomed to making in Venice.

This royal recognition allowed Verzelini a monopoly for that period to make glasses in England, provided he sold them as cheap as, or cheaper than, the foreign products, and with the further proviso that he would teach his skills to the English. Foreign competition was thus eliminated while his patent lasted, and his business prospered to such an extent that under his supervision various glass houses were erected throughout the country.

In the British Museum there still exists a Verzelini goblet inscribed with the diamond point and dated 1586, "In God is All Mi Trust." This must be one of the few identifiable glasses if not the only one still surviving whose origin can be definitely stated. The glass in the goblet is not quite clear but is of a brown, yellowish-green tint, resembling the Venetian glass of the late sixteenth century.

Working about a century later than Verzelini was a notable English glass worker, George Ravenscroft, and his drinking glasses are looked on as among the most interesting of the late seventeenth century productions; any owner of a Ravenscroft glass is much to be envied.

His early glasses suffered from crizzling — a loss of transparency — but later this fault was remedied and he claimed for his glass that it was "hard, durable, and whiter than any from Venice." In an advertisement in the London *Gazette* of October 25, 1677, Ravenscroft stated, "In case any of the above-said glasses shall happen to crizzle or decay as once they did, they shall be readily changed by the said shop-keeper . . . or the money returned to content of the party aggrieved."

Ravenscroft glasses were produced at a glass house in the Savoy London, called the Raven's Head, which used as its device a Raven's Head, and not inappropriately Ravenscroft marked his work with the same emblem.

It is interesting to reflect that because of the drawings of drinking glasses done by Greene and sent to Venice to be copied, it is possible for us to trace the growth of the designs of "Domestic dram glasses" used in the reign of Charles II, and to learn from his "patterns" exactly the type of glasses men drank from in the late sixteen hundreds. This is information which otherwise would almost certainly have been denied to us.

As might be expected those early glasses were simple in conception, the greatest number being of the funnel type, and many were of the original version of the straight-sided bowl — typically an English style. This was produced in the large goblet type and in the smaller, daintier wine glasses.

There was little applied decoration possibly because the workers had not the skill for it, but on certain glasses with a tapered bowl there appeared a raised pattern which looked as if blobs of glass had been super-imposed on the surface. Another form of ornamentation was achieved by making the glasses of ribbed glass; this appeared chiefly on the more capacious types.

Stems were short in the early specimens, none of them equalling half the height of the entire glass, but the designs of the stems which were usually hollow varied to an astonishing degree; and the feet were of the folded variety raised in the center imitating the Venetian styles.

As has been indicated, tumblers lacked appeal but the glass mug, sister to the tumbler, is a delightful piece when it can be found. It was made in the second half of the eighteenth century when workmanship of all the crafts was at its best. It was finely proportioned and often had a fluted base.

It is presumed that one of the reasons for the scarcity of the glass mug is the fact that at that time pewter was frequently used for spirits and being more serviceable than the glass was not so likely to be smashed. It may be worth mentioning the origin of the word "tumbler." This arose from the early design which was made with a rounded base so that it could not stand up. It was therefore a tumbler.

Tumblers made to stand alone without support were introduced in the reign of the first George. While it is rewarding for a collector to come on specimens of early seventeenth-century glasses, it should be remembered that by the beginning of the eighteenth century designs had greatly improved and glasses had become much more decorative. This was an almost obvious happening in an age when the vogue for drinking and gaming parties was at its height, and conviviality and revelry abounded.

In that elegant era more and more attention was being given to producing graceful designs. Glasses became taller with better proportions and the baluster-knopped stem which was noticeable on nearly all the dram glasses of the time added to the importance of the shape.

Made in a variety of patterns the baluster gave a new look to the simplest design, and the taller the glass the more effective was the overall result. Tall glasses with baluster stems and good proportions lent beauty and grace to the dining tables at a time when those qualities were beginning to count for so much. Although they looked much the same, the actual knops on the stems of the glasses were usually dissimilar, each made in a different pattern, however slight.

At the turn of the century, owing to the coming of a king and queen fom Holland, there were signs of Dutch influence. The cultural interests of William and Mary had not only introduced the beauty of Chinese porcelain to the stately homes of England but had also brought from the Low Countries exciting new glass designs. These included the tall baluster stem.

As glass workers learned new secrets in working with glass, decorated glasses began to appear and were swiftly accepted as assets to enhance what had been looked upon as domestic ware. Many forms of ornamentation were thrilling: air bubbles, tears, air twists, filming over the glass with gold leaf, enamelling millefiori glass (one of the oldest kinds of decoration), and perhaps most popular of all the cutting of the surface of the glass — a breathless onrush of beauty.

As drinking glasses were so often used in the soft glow of candlelight they were an obvious choice for the cutter on which to try his skill and as the glass of the bowl was usually thin, to be cut successfully the cutter concentrated on the more robust stem. The glasses were tall, slender and finely proportioned and the knopped facets on the stem suggested an ornamentation which would add to the play of light. The foot of the glass, however, was domed and left plain.

In spite of its charm this graceful glass with its straight or ogee bowl does not seem to have been made in very great numbers and was in vogue for a comparatively short time, from about 1730 to 1750. One of its striking features was the size of the foot which tended to be unusually large in proportion to the small, rather delicate bowl.

It is interesting to study the shape of the bowl in any old drinking glass. Most characteristic of the early designs was the funnel bowl which was rounded and had straight sloping sides with either a square or a rounded base. In the early years of the eighteenth century it was remarkably long in proportion to the stem and it had a simple inverted baluster which occupied most of the stem. Later in the century the bowl was much shorter.

In some of Greene's designs a bowl having straight vertical sides and a square base is frequent, but while this type persisted throughout the eighteenth century it was never so popular as the rounded funnel bowl. The simple baluster stem originated in Venice and was an important feature on English glasses, both the true baluster and the inverted type; both varieties sometimes appeared on the same stem.

With the immigration of German glass workers into England German styles began to appear and the arrival of the waisted bowl was directly due to their influence. It had incurved sides and a flaring rim and though it lacked the appeal of the earlier examples it had a long run of popularity and was in favor for about forty years. It was less common in the second half of the century when it was largely replaced by the straight sided bowl or a simple ogee bowl which could be more easily engraved.

Other designs of the waisted bowl had names which described its shape. There were double ogee types as well as the ale glass bowl which was tall and narrow and was sometimes used as a small cordial glass. On all such glasses the foot is either of the domed type, often having radial ribs rising from the circular base to the stem, or the spreading type. The former shape is the more attractive of the two but unfortunately for collectors it was seldom made after 1740 while the spreading foot was found in most eighteenth-century glasses and in those of the nineteenth century, too.

The two shapes are very similar save that the spreading foot does not incline upwards but rather is flat. It may be noted here that while the domed foot is not comon on drinking glasses it was a usual feature on sweetmeat glasses.

When the art of cutting glass reached England in the second decade of the eighteenth century it lent a new excitement to the possession of glass ware but the art developed slowly in England. Glass cutting had been known to, and practiced by, the Romans but as a decoration it had lapsed over a long period, until the beginning of the seventeenth century when it was rediscovered in Bohemia by one Caspar Lehmann. Before glass cutting was established in England as an industry the English exported various glass articles uncut to the Continent where they were cut or engraved and then sent back to Britain. This habit was discontinued as individual glass cutters learned cutting skills in England.

Cuting on the rims of drinking glasses was an early feature but it had to be stopped for practical reasons, though it was still used as a decoration on the rims of other glasses which were not dram glasses, such as honey jars, bowls and salad bowls. This delightful ornamentation has never gone out of fashion.

Numerous German designs were used in the cutting of glass but the plain flat diamonds which appeared about 1740 and were immediately popular have remained one of the most characteristic devices and are found on most cut glass. Towards the end of the century vertical flutes were in favor and these were employed either alone or in company with flat diamonds. In the last quarter of the century convex diamonds were common, though as it was not suitable for the bowl it had to be confined to the stem. Later, the glass workers evolved flat sliced cutting specially suited to a thin glass.

Glass cutting in England was retarded in the eighteenth century because the full development of the cutting demanded a thick metal, but in 1745 excise duties were imposed on this kind of glass which made it essential from an economic point of view to produce glasses which were small and light. This explains the simplicity of the cutting and the necessity to confine it mainly to the stem. The same Act hit the workers in Ireland where the weight of the glasses was not only reduced, but the export of glass from the country was prohibited altogether.

For a time, in their search for old glasses, collectors tended to ignore cut glass preferring either the simple type of good design, or the glass which owed its appeal to engraving, enamelling or air twist stems, but good cut glass has never lost its charm.

Engraving was a rather earlier decoration than cutting and as with cutting the engravers brought their art from Germany. It must have been a tremendous thrill when domestic users of glass discovered the joys of pieces which were cut or engraved. Delightful as large pieces of glass undoubtedly are, there is something particularly appealing and lovely in the little pieces, whose beauty must have come to life under the glow of candle light.

If engraving made a less spectacular entrance on the English scene (about 1713) than cutting, its very restraint was a joy. At first the German workmen who had made engraving possible introduced their own styles of prim flowers and vine leaves to the bowls of the dram glasses, but after a decade or two, circa 1740, the English began to produce their own designs, which were less formal and stereotyped.

Natural looking wreaths of flowers including roses decorated the bowls of the glasses along with butterflies, birds and insects, and this dainty type of ornamentation gave the glasses their name, and they became known as flower glasses. This was the best period of engraved glass. A more sturdy design of hops and barley succeeded the delicate flower glasses but designs deteriorated considerably during the last quarter of the century.

According to modern taste the engraved glass is interesting but its designs cannot be termed artistic, and one school of thought states that the only acceptable reason for engraving a wine glass is for the purpose of displaying the crest or coat of arms of its owner. However, a finely engraved border done in an early style, round the top edge of the bowl, supplies a most pleasing decoration.

Another use for the engraved glass was to celebrate some event or personage in history by engraving the bowl in some fashion. The Jacobite Rebellion was responsible for a crop of commemorative glasses showing the crowned head of Prince Charles Edward, and examples of this type of glass were made in memory of the two sides in a dynastic conflict — the House of Hanover and the exiled House of Stuart with the cipher I.R. and mottoes, loyal verses and a crown scratched on the glass with the diamond point.

For collectors these are probably the most interesting of the engraved specimens. Another is the banqueting goblet. This was first made towards the end of the seventeenth century when glass was scarce and dear, and one drinking glass had to be shared among several guests and then, as each one drank from it in turn as from a loving cup, it was passed round the table. This was an outsize goblet but it was produced in small numbers and is therefore extremely rare.

Though not of themselves intrinsically attractive, old Masonic glasses are also of interest. They were made during the second half of the seventeenth century when the Masonic movement was so popular. They had a straight tapered bowl and while they were lacking in grace their appearance conveyed their purpose — glasses intended for drinking purposes.

The Masonic glass had no stem and the bowl rested on a double foot of extreme thickness, said to have been designed so that the glass could withstand the loud rapping on the table after a toast had been drunk. Such glasses often had emblems of the craft with which the members were connected — and also the Lodge with which they were associated — engraved on the bowl. Masonic glasses were never small but sometimes they were very large and were reputed to hold a quart of liquor on high, festive occasions.

Beginners who are anxious to aquire some engraved glasses, perhaps on a holiday when buying tends to be more casual, should try to obtain a guarantee that the piece is what it is stated to be, and that the date is at least approximately correct. Many glasses may indeed have been made about the date indicated, but the engraving may have been added at a later date, even a century after the glass was originally made, and this detracts from the value.

During the middle years of the eighteenth century the dram glass with the air twist stem was produced, a form of ornamentation which came about accidentally in the early years of the century when tears or bubbles were discovered in the actual manufacture of the glass. The result was so effective that the glass makers explored the possibilities and the air twist was cultivated in a host of different patterns.

The twists themselves form endless designs having the air threads thick or thin by which the most complex designs appear. Double and treble twists combine and opaque threads and air threads all blend together with hardly any repetition in the general finish. Those with air twists are among the most coveted in the old English glasses and though they are now scarce they are still obtainable.

Sometimes the knop in the stem is filled with bubbles and another graceful effect is the drawn or trumpet air bowl; there is occasionally a coin found inserted in the stem and less frequently a button or "prunt."

It is interesting to note how the white threads in the stem vary from a hair's breadth to the

Two large Bristol goblets. Not a pair. *Circa* 1795. (Courtesy John Bell)

knop. But this is not a frequent occurance as by that time the knopped glass was beginning to go out of favor.

White opaque enamelling on the bowls is very rare and while the effect is rather heavy when it does appear, such glasses are so scarce that they command high prices. Conventional scrolls are common as are vine leaves and grapes, or there may be a tiny landscape picked out in a silhouette of white enamel. An interesting point is that straight sided and ogee bowls are generally of English origin; bell-shaped bowls however were made on the Continent in large numbers and many were exported to England.

One type of old drinking glass which is neither elegant nor decorative should not be ignored. This is the tavern glass which was of a simple design, without ornamentation. As its name suggests it was meant to be strong enough to stand up to the wear and tear of usage in a public tavern, and it was also used as an everyday glass in the home.

width of a solid "tape" of cord, and every kind of twist is covered by a coating of clear glass which also varies in thickness.

Throughout the century air twist glasses became more elaborate and included both white and colored enamels and there was an ever increasing change in design. Many of the colored threads are believed to have come from Bristol where so much beautiful colored glass was made, notably the famous blue Bristol and the rich red Bristol.

When enamel twists are present they usually occupy the greater part of the stem interior, but this is not always so and occasionally one comes on a kind of loose twist inside the stem which is unexpectedly attractive. It is surprising that the colored twists were not made in larger quantities as they can create an effect which is quite dramatic, much more so than the white twist.

It should perhaps be emphasized that air twist glasses belong not merely to the expensive group of drinking glasses but to the connoisseur glass. In addition to this they are rare and the choice of types of twist is fast diminishing. From any angle they are not the kind of glass to be casually picked up.

The stems of cordial glasses in which air twists are found are usually slender and are otherwise undecorated, but in those specimens made about 1750 there is a double baluster or perhaps a single

Heavily cut glass compote, eighteenth century. High stepped lid. (Courtesy John Bell)

Such glasses should not be despised because of their modest qualities as they have a certain rugged charm of their own, and a search in some remote Inn or out-of-the-way antiques shop may bring to light the odd plain glass dating back to the early seventeen hundreds. At the same time it must be appreciated that the glass used to make them was of tavern quality and hardly fit to be used in company with really fine glass.

While drinking glasses were intended to hold any kind of liquor some fine glasses were produced for special drinks. Ale for instance was drunk from glasses in which the most characteristic note was their design, particularly the size and shape of the bowl. This was a straight sided drawn bowl made in an elongated style. Some ale glasses were so long that they were referred to as yard glasses.

Tumblers as we know them today were made from about the first quarter of the eighteenth century but the most desirable period was from 1750 to 1760. They were rather small, were made to taper slightly, and were sometimes engraved with roses, but these are by no means plentiful.

Beer mugs and tankards were made in large quantities throughout the hospitable days of the latter half of the eighteenth century. Some of these were very attractive, finely proportioned and designed; some were decorated and others plain; and some specimens had a fluted base. Nowadays these are not easy to come by. Glass tankards are also rare and unfortunately many of the tankards are coarse, of the quality made for the tavern and not the kind of glass likely to appeal to the average collector.

Champagne glasses were widely produced in the eighteenh century though it is questionable whether they were designed specially for this wine or were intended as sweetmeat glasses. But the fact that many of those early glasses were made with a serrated lip on the bowl appears to deny this as a shape that would be more suited to a sweetmeat container than a glass which would come in contact with the mouth.

However, the type which was supposed to have been made especially for champagne was produced only until about 1760, though some authorities quote an earlier date. It had a large flat open bowl with an outline that was most gracefully

Eighteenth-century mead glass with waisted bowl and Jacobite engraving. Knopped circular base. (Courtesy Arthur Churchill)

curved with a domed foot and frequently a knopped stem. Air buble groups, fine air twists and white spirals are among the features of the eighteenth-century champagne glasses. They usually had some kind of decoration and invariably they were stately and beautiful.

A most unusual find is the cider glass. It has a tall slender stem and a foot that is gently domed, but the most attractive part is the bowl which is straight-sided and hardly tapers at all so that it is almost rectangular in shape. Cider glasses were made from about 1750 onwards, and there was fine engraving on the bowls of some examples, with designs of apples and apple trees and of cider barrels. Some of these were carried out in oil gilt and were very effective.

One of the most rare glasses is the small Scottish thistle glass which was first made at the end of the eighteenth century. In spite of its intriguing appearance it did not remain long in production owing to its design. This was planned with a bulge at the base which made it difficult to drain at one gulp and customers at taverns complained that the measure was short. Manufacturers ceased to make it and consequently original thistle glasses are not often to be had.

It is not easy to identify the date of dram or cordial glasses, but the pontil mark can act as a guide to the age of a wine glass. The pontil is a small, sharp excrescence which can be felt by the finger on the base when the glass is turned up. This feature was found on all glasses made until the end of the eighteenth century. It was caused when the bowl was being made — the glass being held in position by means of an iron rod, called the pontil, attached to the bottom of the glass.

When the making of the glass was completed the pontil was detached by a sharp blow on the rod and this left a protruding roughness which was called the pontil mark. In the early years of the following century the finish was mechanized

Set of finely engraved goblet size wine glasses with smaller sherry glasses to match. (Courtesy John Bell)

so that the base of the glass was perfectly smooth with no hint of roughness.

It is natural that in an age when there was so much eating and drinking and showing hospitality on a wide scale, much table glass ware should have been produced. In addition to the numerous drinking glasses there were many other small beautiful pieces which found their way to the dining table. In the early years of the nineteenth century particularly there was a great display of finely cut glass, made both in Ireland and in England.

Among the most enchanting of these were sweetmeat glasses. Authorities differ as to when they were made and while some writers place their initial appearance at the time of Queen Anne, others put the date several decades later.

The likeness between certain specimens of sweetmeat glasses and champagne glasses has already been referred to, and while opinions differ many of those early glasses with a thick undulating edge may be reasonably classed as having been intended for sweetmeats rather than for champagne.

A feature of the sweetmeat glasses is the domed foot, which is an almost invariable finish It is always small and lends an agreeable touch. Another characteristic is the fact that the glasses stood high and were very lovely as well as stately. Until about 1760 they were made with a large open bowl with a gracefully curved outline sometimes of the ogee type.

Until the middle of the century cutting was rarely seen on such glasses, but from then on it became an accepted decoration. The bowls of the glasses differed very much in shape. Sometimes one was fashioned like a tulip not fully opened, another looked like a tulip with serrated edges deeply indented, while a third graceful bowl had an edge that was only modestly serrated.

Now and again the bowl had a smooth uncut edge and might have been used as a drinking glass, but it was more often shallower than the accepted champagne glass. The bowls rested on tall stems which were beautifully cut and the cutting was frequently repeated on the domed foot in a widely varying number of patterns. The most usual type of cutting on early sweetmeat glasses showed the scalloped edge, and this decorative treatment on the rim of the bowl and around the foot added con-

Two early glass sweetmeat dishes with serrated dog tooth rims, white baluster shaped spirals. Period *c.* 1720. (Courtesy John Bell)

Two Victorian sweetmeat glasses with serrated edges and tapering sides. (Courtesy John Bell)

Fine Waterford pickle jar with lid. Beautifully cut, lozenge-shaped finial. Square base. (Courtesy John Bell)

siderably to the grace of the piece. A richly cut sweetmeat glass with a scalloped rim, a drawn and faceted stem, and a domed foot with a scalloped rim, glittering in the soft candlelight must have been an enchanting sight.

Pickle jars were also most pleasing. The most typical style was the urn shape with fine cutting both on the body and on the raised base which was usually circular, but was sometimes square with a stepped finish. The jar with the very slender body which stands high and has a domed lid which rises to a pointed stopper is particularly graceful. This type is often decorated with versica cutting.

A feature of the pickle jar was the domed lid and the cut-glass stopper, and there was often additional cutting on the edge of the body. With the advent of the nineteenth century the proportions were less pleasing. The lid lost its height and grace and was inclined to be too heavy in comparison with the bowl, and while the workmanship remained good, the cutting lacked the elegance of the earlier jars.

Some beautiful little jars made in the eighteenth century were of Irish origin and were made in Cork. Other table pieces, also of Irish manufacture,

Irish glass preserves jar, eighteenth century. Fine hobnail cutting, made *c.* 1795. (Courtesy John Bell)

A beautiful pair of Irish Waterford custard cups lavishly cut. (Courtesy John Bell)

Butter cooler on stand. Very richly cut. Deeply serrated edges. (Courtesy John Bell)

were wide-lipped cream jugs with a generously curved handle, and sugar basins of a plain circular design, with a sometimes matching lid. While the base of this kind of sugar basin rested firmly on the table, some examples were linked by a short stem to a circular base, and on such simple pieces the cutting was important. Nailhead diamonds and also prismatic cutting around the neck of the cream jug were frequent.

Other eighteenth century small pieces were butter coolers, in vogue towards the end of the century, and these were designed with a fairly shallow bowl and straight sides and were finished with a narrow upstanding serrated collar. This was surmounted by a rather high domed lid and a neat glass stopper. Butter coolers showed a certain diversity in cutting. The most attractive type has a shallow bowl with a wavy edge and a rigid pattern in cutting.

Celery glasses belong to the same era or to a slightly later period. They were popular in the early decades of the nineteenth century, circa 1820–1830. Waterford glass was used for these and a good design had a deep bowl linked to a domed foot by a very short stem. In this the cutting was discrete and was confined to the bowl. There was sometimes a shell-shaped edge allied to a criss-cross de-

sign with more subdued cutting at the base of the bowl.

A simpler design has a bowl which is shorter in length and a slightly modified longer baluster stem. There is prismatic rib cutting near the base and again a serrated edge on the bowl. This is a type which is still in favor today.

Honey pots which had a certain resemblance to

pickle jars were usually circular in shape and were fitted with a glass stopper lid, either flat or rounded. As a variation from the plain round bowl there was sometimes a distinct "waist" occurring where the domed lid rested on the rim of the bowl. Nailhead diamond cutting was frequent on the body with radial ribs on the circular base and the bowl was joined to the foot either by a simple knop or by a slight, short protuberance which was more like an extension of the body than an actual stem.

About 1750 when the pleasure of tea drinking was beginning to be appreciated by a widening circle, the glass tea caddy emerged as a popular adjunct to table accessories. It was an elegant piece, in appearance resembling a perfume bottle with a simple stopper. It was small, as tea was still an expensive commodity. It was more often engraved than cut and bore the name of the tea in the center of the jar — Bohea, Indian, Green, surrounded by an ornametnal design. For about a decade, between 1760 and 1770, Bristol turned out extremely decorative caddies made of opaque white (tin) glass.

Cut glass sugar casters were in use at a comparatively early date. Examples made in the latter half of the eighteenth century, from 1760 onward, had a graceful body which became rather full towards the circular base. Those casters had pierced mounts of silver topped by a delicately designed finial.

Amid the glittering array of glass which added lustre and gaiety to the dining room and elsewhere about the house, it is not surprising that candlesticks were prominent. Silver candlesticks and candelabra were used by those who could afford them but the charm of a small single candlestick was universally admitted.

Candlesticks belonging to the second half of the eighteenth century are very desirable. Stems which often showed a modified baluster were slender and scalloped rims of both feet and nozzles were a feature of this period. It is interesting also to note that while the domed foot in wine glasses had by this time almost disappeared it continued in most candlesticks.

A simple inverted baluster stem was found on some early candlesticks before cutting was introduced, but this was an ungainly style which did not prove popular and few examples of this have survived.

The high domed foot lent considerable importance to the candlestick and this was often emphasized by radial ribs and a spreading effect when the dome was gradual. This was very decorative especially when it was allied to a stem with a double baluster. Stems with diamond facets and vertical cutting date from about 1770 and sometimes on candlesticks made about that time there was scalloping on both rims and nozzles. On earlier types cutting was usually confined to the stem and the nozzles were plain.

There was a vogue for cut glass table candlesticks in the early nineteenth century. These showed the classical influence and while they lacked the severe beauty of those made in the previous century they possessed a distinct charm. The body was slender

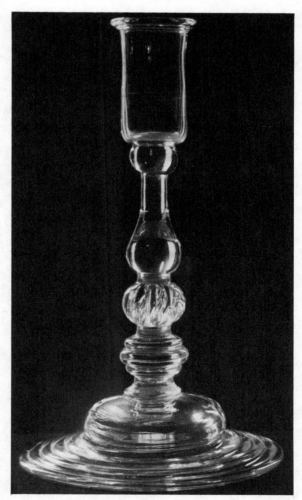

Candlestick with knopped stem and circular stepped base. (Courtesy Arthur Churchill)

and in shape resembled an urn mounted on a square-stepped base and above the neck of the stem there was a wide scalloped tray from which were suspended six or eight pendant lustres, usually diamond or pear shaped. The nozzle had a scalloped edge and when the candles were lit the effect must have been delightful.

Later in the century candlesticks with pendant lustres were exaggerated in every way, with a wider tray, longer and fussier drops, presenting an over elaborate effect and consequently a lack of grace.

3

From the Stool to the Chair

Looking back with the advantages of hindsight it seems almost incredible that the chair took so long to establish itself as an essential piece of domestic furniture. Next in importance to possessing something "from which to eat and something to lie on" surely must come something for the individual to sit on. But until the close of the Middle Ages chairs were so rarely found in the average home that they were practically non-existent.

Towards the end of the fourteenth century and about the beginning of the fifteenth, mention of a few chairs began to creep into the Inventories of the time, but even in the baronial castles and great houses of the nobles, they were greatly outnumbered by the "shared" type of seating, benches, forms, and settles, and it was well into the reign of the first Elizabeth before they appeared to any extent in Wills.

Life at that time was in many ways a communal business, and when it came to providing seating accommodation there was for a very long time no question of supplying any sort of separate seat for individuals. Apart from a few exceptions men and women of all classes of society in the thirteenth and fourteenth centuries were accustomed to sit on the same seat as other occupants of their homes — on a settle or bench or a chest. These were accepted as the only possible type of seat.

It should be understood that the chest of those days was not a chest with drawers but a deep long box with a lid. It was usually made of oak and it was designed to fulfill the functions of a trunk or a piece for storing various possessions, but because of its shape and its convenient height, approximately the same as a settle, it was recognized as a suitable seat.

When the first chairs appeared they were looked on as the most important piece of furniture, intended for ceremonial occasions only; and for a long time, until about the seventeenth century, they were kept for the use of the master of the house and for distinguished visitors.

Gradually the number of chairs increased. The chair made a niche for itself but its progress was slow. As late as 1542 "The Vine," a mansion of 52 rooms owned by the then Lord Sandys, had only 19 chairs listed among its contents. Not even a chair for every two rooms. And an Inventory of a mansion of the same period might have only one or two chairs. In one such home one of those few chairs is reputed to have been kept solely for the master, save on the rare occasions when the king, Henry VIII, honored the family with a visit, and it was then occupied by the royal guest.

As time went on the mistress of the household was elevated by possessing a chair for herself, and in 1580 a most sumptuous chair, richly carved and having her initials A M carved on the back, was specially made for Annabella Countess of Mar. It was she whose husband was Regent during the minority of James VI of Scotland and I of the United Kingdom, the son of Mary Queen of Scots, so that in the absence of a reigning monarch she was the first lady of the land.

It is fascinating to trace the growth of the chair. The earliest type was a modification of the lidded chest or box and so was called a box chair. The seat was actually a square, deep box; it was stout and strong and it acted as a container for household goods, including books. The back was panelled and the side arm rests acted as supports for the long hanging sleeves which were modish in the fifteenth century.

This early design was often called "a close or joyn'd chayre" and it was made up until the sixteenth century in which century it was followed by

Regency chair with delicately turned legs. Curved and reeded arms, and finely carved back. (Courtesy John Bell)

the graceful X-chair so called because it was formed like a curved X. For a seat it had a piece of fabric stretched across it and it was decorated with linenfold panelling. It is said that Princess Mary, daughter of Henry VIII, used a chair like this when she married Phillip of Spain.

About the same era there appeared the Glastonbury chair — a most revolutionary design as it was made on similar lines to the modern camp chair. It had a carved panelled back and carved sloping arms and its enormous advantage was that it could be folded when not in use, and when people of quality travelled around the country paying the long visits which they undertook despite the difficulties of road and transport they could include their own chair in their luggage.

After the Glastonbury came the high-backed carved oak chair which was much used in churches and not so much in private homes. But chronologically it is the stool which takes precedence over the chair. The date of its origin is uncertain but long before the chair was thought of it had joined the other few domestic pieces of furniture then in existence.

It is known to have been in use during the Middle Ages and almost certainly before that. The three-legged stool seems to have been the earliest type and it is not impossible that its long life may have begun in the byre where servants and milkmaids discovered the convenience of the design and the coarse scrubbed wood.

Undoubtedly the stool was part of the furnishings in the time of the Tudors, and Shakespeare in *Cymbeline* (Act III, scene 3) makes Belanno say, "When on my three legged stool I sit." It was succeeded in the sixteenth century by a small rectangular oak stool which looked like a miniature refectory table with shaped ends and a flat solid stretcher.

Later in the century the stool again resembled a little dining table of oak, this time a copy of the Elizabethan table with turned legs and stretchers, and a panelled top which protruded a little over the under framing. This marked the introduction of a cabinet maker's stool, a great improvement on the earlier work by the joiner. It was a handsome piece, well constructed and decorated and it continued to be produced until the end of the seventeenth cen-

Oak seventeenth-century stool. Shaped sides, turned legs and stretchers. (Courtesy John Bell)

Charming low set stool. Seventeenth century. Upholstered top with deep galon fringe. Turned legs and stretchers. (Courtesy John Bell)

tury, when its qualities commended it to those people of more modest means as well as to the aristocrats.

But the dawn of the eighteenth century affected the stool in two opposite directions. In one way its growth was retarded by the increasing popularity of the chairs which were swiftly becoming fashionable, and in that sense the mode seemed to be killing the stool. But against that the many fine stools scattered in the homes about the land could not be scrapped forthwith and they were retained for casual use in the bedroom or hall.

In this different guise the stool took on a new and intriguing look, as if it were almost a fresh invention. The chief difference wrought by the cabinet makers of the day was to pad it for comfort so that it gave the impression of being required for a seat to be sat on for a period of time.

Many new and exciting pieces came into being during the reign of Queen Anne but it is hard to think of any that surpass in elegance and charm the walnut stool of that period. Rectangular in shape with cabriole legs and stretchers, most richly carved and finely upholstered, it was a pleasing asset to any

room in the house. Some of its notable features were the claw feet and the carved masks on the knees and frame.

Even though it was so luxurious an item the upholstered stool was not the beginning of the padded seat, for during the Protectorate in the middle years of the seventeenth century seats and backs were upholstered in leather and fastened to the frame of the chair by little brass nails closely placed together. Also there were upholstered arm chairs about a hundred years earlier, at the beginning of that century at the time of King James I of the United Kingdom.

By the end of the seventeenth century upholstery on English chairs was becoming an accepted part of their construction. Their seats and backs were padded tapestry, velvet, or damask, sometimes finished with a galon or fringe and attached to the frame as the brass nails had been to the earlier chairs.

When the Queen Anne stool appeared it also was finished with a fairly deep fringe which hid the wood of the frame. Tapestry was a favorite occupation of the women of those days and the most beautiful stools bore evidence of their skill and industry. In rare cases one still finds a Queen Anne stool with its original stitchery, faded and perhaps a little worn but still carrying the remnants of its one time beauty.

Pleasing little pair of fruitwood stools with loose upholstered tops. Square tapered legs. (Courtesy John Bell)

Tapestry was the most enduring of all coverings but many richer fabrics such as brocades, heavy silks, and even stiff satins as well as wool embroidery were also used. Stools of this period were made in walnut, a wood which lent itself to a refinement of treatment in a way that oak did not. It was therefore not only the obvious choice but the only one suitable as mahogany did not come into general use for domestic furniture until about 1715. Until then it was scarce in England and was used sparingly, mainly as a veneer.

Following these lovely Queen Anne stools came a simpler type. They were still in walnut and had the cabriole leg though in a more modified form; they had pad feet and restrained carving at the knee and in the center of the frame. They lacked

Delightful Queen Anne walnut stool upholstered in contemporary needlework. Cabriole legs richly carved on the knees and feet. (Courtesy M. Harris)

Delightful pair of small Georgian stools on shaped cabriole legs. Upholstered in wool needlework. (Courtesy John Bell)

the stretchers of the earlier variety and were often a little lower in height. While less elaborate than their fore-runners they too were covered in rich upholstery and small brass nails were again in fashion as an attachment.

Attractive as those Georgian stools were they had not the delectable charm of the Queen Anne specimens which are now rare. The Queen Anne varieties are often employed nowadays as dressing stools as are the Georgian stools. Any one of those early stools is a treasured legacy but it is easier to acquire a mahogany stool which gradually and surprisingly superceded the walnut specimens though these continued to be made.

Among the mahogany examples, the more pleasing have straight grooved legs joined by stretchers. Some of the Chippendale styles popular about the middle of the century show a suggestion of Chippendale's love of Eastern designs, such as spandrils carved in Oriental fashion linking the under framing with the leg.

Most of the stools of that time were almost severely plain and were a striking contrast to the curves and carving of the elaborate Queen Anne styles;

but it should be remembered that for the greater part of the preceding two centuries oak had been the chief wood. Designs of chair legs had been elaborate — very bulky in the Elizabethan era preceeding the barley sugar twists of the Charles and Protectorate times.

One must not forget that mahogany was a new wood demanding fresh treatment, hence the combination of straight lines with no applied ornament whatever. Partly because of that the new designs were most acceptable. Seen now, objectively the plain mahogany stool has stood the test of time and will stand happily beside furniture of almost any age without loss of charm.

The next change was the drop-in seat. It was the beginning of the vogue for loose covers on the chairs and matching curtains, chiefly in bedrooms but also in drawing rooms, and it has been suggested that the drop-in seat on the stool was introduced to facilitate laundering, as washing materials were coming into fashion. A feature of the drop-in seat was that it was encircled by wood which helped to display the mahogany of the frame.

Some authorities give credit to Hepplewhite for the idea of the drop-in seat. He it was who considered the needs of the middle classes and introduced practical designs. This was in contrast to Chippendale who worked always with the preferences of the aristocracy before him. It is by no means certain that Hepplewhite was the originator however, and other writers claim that it was Robert Adam who introduced the notion.

Fashion even in furniture is never static and even at the height of the popularity of the plain mahogany stool there was a reversion to the walnut type with modified cabriole legs. Carving of shells at the knees was also in favor for a time though this stool was not so effective as the first walnut stools. The design was not so good and the coverings less sumptuous.

By the second half of the eighteenth century the output of the stool had increased, making it quite important. While numerically it did not equal the number of chairs being made it was produced by all the eminent cabinet makers of the day and while the basic design of all the stools was faultless, styles altered with the passing of time — in the woods used, in the designs submitted by the different craftsmen, and by small details. Because of this it is not always possible to date an eighteenth-century stool to within a decade or two.

It has, however, remained a desirable piece, and while the later varieties cannot compare with the Queen Anne stool in elegance it still makes a most pleasing addition to almost any room in the house. Coverings, whether washable or belonging to the richer material, were delightfully colorful. Among the materials which could be laundered dimity was coming into fashion. Chintz too was popular.

About 1760 there were some slight variations in the severity of the mahogany stool. One was the introduction by Chippendale of a seat rail allied to square legs carved in the Chinese taste, an extension of the Oriental ideas which he liked so much and which he had already used on many of his designs. Another alteration was the combination of slightly fluted legs and stretchers allied to the drop-in seat, but this had only a brief popularity.

Although they are not characteristic of the eighteenth century styles the small rectangular oak stools with turned legs and stretchers and panelled tops popular in the sixteenth and seventeenth centuries continued to be made, chiefly it is supposed by country cabinet makers working in remote areas where furniture fashions changed slowly. Many such stools were still in existence and were much

Hepplewhite mahogany stool with upholstered drop-in seat. Straight legs and stretchers. (Courtesy John Bell)

valued by their possessors who added a note of color to their appearance by way of a loose linen cushion — green, blue or ruby — placed on top and attached to the seat by tapes.

Hepplewhite stools are unspectacular. Rectangular in shape with slender legs, these were usually straight in the fashion of the time but might be curved a little or splayed. It was Hepplewhite who brought back the three-legged stool with its circular upholstered top; he also re-introduced the cabriole leg in a simplified manner.

Another design attributed to Hepplewhite is the gouty stool. This reflected the need to support the feet as a result of the prevalence of gout, one of the most frequent illnesses of the day. It was rectangular with square legs and it was so designed that it could be adjusted to the most comfortable angle for the relief of the aching foot. Sheraton also made a gouty stool. It was more elaborate than the one made by Hepplewhite and could be raised to a considerable height, but it could be folded down into a comparatively small space when not required.

The Victorian stools must not be overlooked. It is only recently that Victoriana of any kind has been accepted as antique and even now few of the best of the London dealers consider pieces to be antique if they were made after 1830. To any one seriously interested in antiques the reason for this is obvious. After the end of the Regency period which may be taken as approximately 1820, or some years later (for one furnishing period tends to overlap into the one following it), good taste, which had been degenerating since the beginning of the nineteenth century, now underwent a sharp collapse.

The refined clean-cut lines and the excellence of the designs of the earlier eighteenth-century pieces were now looked on as being out of date and were replaced by new furniture which lacked altogether the good styles that had been in vogue for so long. The Victorians were living in an affluent society and in a desire to express their comfortable circumstances they seemed to throw off the restraint which had been so delightful a feature of the eighteenth-century craftsmen.

The cabinet makers responded to their wishes just as the cabinet makers of the early eighteenth century had fallen into line with the customers of that time, and they produced furniture which was fussy and over elaborate but which produced the desired result in that it looked expensive and in keeping with the status in life of the purchasers.

Into this background of costly inelegance there came the stool. An anachronism if ever there was one, for the stool was everything which the Victorian furniture was not — modest, self-effacing, simple in design and quietly pleasing. A proof of its good lines is that it can be placed alongside eighteenth-century pieces without losing caste, and without appearing to be slightly uncultured, a statement which can be applied to a minimum of Victorian pieces only. It appears to be exactly what it is, a simple, practical seat of good design and faultless workmanship.

Stools of that era were made in different sizes, but there are three main sizes, the smallest being the little circular footstool. In that leisured age, when women were occupied by much letter writing and by their needlework skill, a little footstool was a pleasant indulgence. The frame of the stool was usually of mahogany or rosewood, but sometimes the fruit woods were used. On this was mounted an upholstered top which consisted most frequently of wool tapestry or of tapestry combined with beadwork and in the better examples the beadwork predominated. Subdued coloring was used for this as a rule, but occasionally there was a background of bright green or orange.

It was a low stool standing a few inches only from the floor and it rested on three, or even four tiny bun feet. From the practical point of view the top which is sewn in wool without any beadwork is the type to look for as the pressure of the feet on the beadwork causes the beads to become detached, and while the beadwork stands up very well with care it may lose its tenure, and anyone who has tried to re-embroider any loose beads will appreciate the difficulty of this task.

In the trio of Victorian stools the other two were square in shape and had four legs, usually of mahogany. The smaller of the two was fairly low, standing about a foot from the floor and was used as a fireside stool. It had an upholstered top and a frequent cover was in heavy velvet of a darkish shade; dull red or green were popular. This was sometimes finished with a deep fringe to match the background of the upholstery. When the fringe was lacking there was a broad band of mahogany binding the frame, and when the base of the band was reeded it made a decorative finish.

There is a tendency just now for possessors of Victorian stools to replace a velvet top with one of tapestry, but a more suitable finish would be one of dull brocade or even a plain modern velvet.

The third stool is similar in appearance to this latter variety save that it is higher, about 15 inches or so from the floor, barely as high as an ordinary chair. The most characteristic treatment of this stool is a dull plush velvet with a colored fringe, or alternately a wool tapestry top sewn against a background of bright wool. This may be allied to a design of beadwork in quieter shades.

A typical scheme might have a floral center of white, grey, brown and black beads, embroidered against a background of orange-colored tapestry, and finished round the edge; that is, at right angles to the top, with a band of soft velvet to tone with the wool background, and kept in place by a narrow strip of galon.

It is when one comes across a gay combination of vivid colors that one realizes how effective the Victorian conception may be. Victorian stools are astonishingly good mixers against a modern scheme providing a striking note of color without any suggestion of disharmony. This even when the wool tapestry is worked in colors which we would term hard, for the crudeness has mellowed with time while the appeal of the color still remains.

Attic treasures of the Victorian era are fast diminishing but any stool of that period should not be discarded without careful consideration. In most rooms a space can be found for the undemanding stool. It may be added that sentiment should not play too great a part in any question of retaining the original upholstery. Better to have a cover not strictly in period but that is attractive and in good color rather than cling to something which "does nothing" for the room.

But there are two schools of thought about this. There is the collector who collects because of the snob value attached to having one's home furnished in antique, and who sets about acquiring old pieces because there is a certain cachet attached to their possession.

Not only does such an attitude result in a furnishing scheme that fails to achieve the best effect, but it does not suggest that the furniture has been selected because of an appreciation of its charm. It may sound like an exaggeration but antiques which have been chosen with affectionate care do come to be loved by their owners. They should not only belong with the rest of the furniture, they should appear to belong.

Space in a modern flat is usually so limited that the acquisition of old chairs must of necessity be very carefully thought out. Any idea of searching for a set of matching chairs for the dining room, or for a dining-sitting room, is almost out of the question. This need not be entirely a matter of regret, and from the financial angle it may even be one of satisfaction, as a set of four or six antique chairs will cost considerably more than four or six times the price of one single chair, of the same type and period.

Viewed from an artistic point of view the odd non-matching chair should not be looked on as a second best. While it may not match in design the other chairs in the room, it must have some affinity with its companions. It need not necessarily be of the same wood but the color should tone. Most woods fade after years of exposure to sun and light and mahogany loses its unattractive reddish hue and takes on a browny shade reminiscent of leather.

So far as color goes, walnut wears best. It takes on a rich golden brown which is quite delightful. Birch too can be most pleasing as by the time it has passed its 200th birthday its color becomes mellow and it bears a close resemblance to mahogany, especially if it has stood in a sunny corner. Chairs made of these different woods and of other woods, including fruit woods and rosewood, will settle beside each other very happily, always provided they are of the same period.

To revert to the question of placing chairs of varying woods in the same room, so long as they tone in color, there may be an exception to this in the case of oak. The dark shade of say a seventeenth-century chair is almost sure to lighten with the years so that it acquires a honey color that is closely akin to the color of an eighteenth-century piece in mahogany.

But oak is of a very different texture from the finer mahogany and this applies also to walnut. These woods are made in different styles from the oak and they do not usually blend well together.

But there are exceptions and an oak chair of the eighteenth century may contradict this rule. Country cabinet makers accustomed to working in oak studied the new designs of the great craftsmen — Chippendale, Hepplewhite, Adam and the others — from books rather than from the actual furniture these men had made. Sometimes they copied the designs exactly but made a change in the wood. The writer has seen a pleasing armchair similar to the chairs produced by Chippendale save that it was made in oak instead of mahogany.

It was put in a room in company with examples of work by the contemporary cabinet makers which were in mahogany, and the effect was quite harmonious though the oak was fundamentally different from the other wood.

In most households odd chairs have survived from bygone generations. Indeed this era might be said to be the century of the casual chair. Never was it so easy to place in almost any room. A dining room with a set of those harlequin chairs can be quite charming.

Suites of furniture — one might almost say suites of anything — are no longer fashionable. This state has arisen because of the lack of space in the modern house or flat. It certainly releases ideas which a generation or two ago were much more hidebound.

In the nineteenth century it was considered good taste to flank each side of the chimney piece with matching ornaments. Today ornaments are rarely displayed in pairs. A Dresden shepherdess may stand at one end of the mantelpiece and a piece of colored glass at the opposite end, the one bearing no apparent relation to the other.

Nearly all chairs made in the eighteenth century will blend with modern surroundings provided they are carefully placed. One possible exception is the Chinese Chippendale chair. While its design is a masterpiece of elegant distinction it has outstanding Oriental features, such as an elaborately pierced back and numerous Chinese touches, that these tend to draw attention to its own superb qualities diminishing the charm of other pieces. For an average room and a modest background the more conventional style is to be preferred.

Sheraton chairs are extremely adaptable, but they do not always rest happily beside others of their own period. In contrast to those specimens made by Chippendale, Hepplewhite and Adam, which suggest a certain solidity, this quality is lacking in the appearance of those turned out by Sheraton. His chairs are so dainty and fragile looking that they give the impression of not being strong enough to stand up to the wear and tear of everyday life. This is inaccurate. Sheraton chairs show markedly the French influence of design and craftsmanship; they are essentially graceful and feminine in appearance but the construction is so skillful that in spite of their slender lines they are so cleverly conceived that they are both strong and durable. They show up best in a bedroom or in a drawing-room.

Although much of Sheraton's work was done in mahogany and to a lesser degree in walnut, his originality came to the fore in his specialization of satinwood whose rich golden tone appealed to his passion for color. Along with inlay he painted his furniture — a popular decoration. He also brought back the cane seat to favor which had been out of fashion since the seventeenth century.

Sheraton designs were a complete breakaway from those of his contemporary cabinet makers. His most typical chair backs were narrow with a straight top rail varied by a geometrically correct crest rail. Some were high with a solid splat across the top while others had more slender splats either horizontal or perpendicular with an intervening design.

He also brought back the turned leg after a lapse of many decades. A badly turned leg can destroy an otherwise beautiful piece, as is evident from a study of Victorian furniture; but in Sheraton's hands the proportions were infallible, and he showed the chair in a new light, slender and tapering, giving it an arresting note of refinement.

Certain types of chairs demand careful placing and one of these is the ladder back. When it was first made it had a country origin and was intended for a cottage or farmhouse, and was therefore pro-

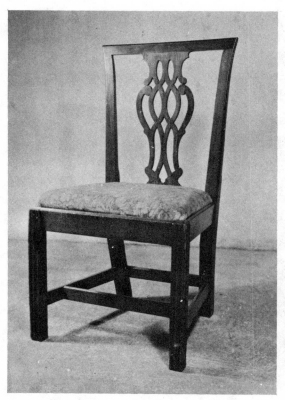

Single Chippendale chair with finely pierced back and stretchers. (Courtesy John Bell)

Hepplewhite armchair with typically designed back and arms that slope back. Straight legs and stretchers. (Courtesy John Bell)

Dainty Sheraton armchair. Straight legs but no stretchers. Back composed of perpendicular slender turned slats. (Courtesy John Bell)

Excellent example of the Adam wheel back chair. Well proportioned. Front legs slender and turned. (Courtesy John Bell)

Sheraton mahogany music chair. Graceful latticed back, upholstered seat and turned legs. (Courtesy John Bell)

duced in the less fine woods, pine, oak or beech. Although it is not quite in character with much of his other furniture it is attributed by some authorities to Chippendale.

In appearance it is like many chairs made in the middle years of the eighteenth century with straight reeded legs and stretchers. The early examples had rush-bottomed seats while as the name implies the back consisted of several horizontal splats set in like the rungs of a ladder. In later specimens they were made in a wavy line which was also very pleasing.

The rush bottom was gradually replaced by an upholstered seat and this is more in keeping with the ideas of Chippendale, and some people think it may have been he who decided to raise the ladder back chair socially by making some examples in mahogany suitable for a town house. But somehow this change was not so successful as was anticipated

Windsor chair of the eighteenth century. Shaped seat and turned legs. (Courtesy John Bell)

and the frankly country ladder back in oak or pine is the more attractive.

The Windsor chair also requires some care in placing as it too is a country piece. Apart from its pleasing design its chief characteristic is the skill exercised in its shaping, so that without any upholstery it is so subtly planned that it fits the body comfortably without the aid of a cushion or any padding.

At first it was made of ash or elm, but birch and beech — and in the better examples oak — were also used. Old Windsor chairs are in great demand today and with the passing of the years the wood has mellowed into a soft tawny color. The legs and staves in the back are rounded and the effect most pleasing. The chair makers of the time had the right idea when they created the Windsor chair in the country type of wood.

There has been much speculation as to the origin of the name of this chair. One version is that King George III and his Queen Charlotte, when in residence at Windsor, admired such a chair in the making at a nearby workshop and gave an order for

Lovely mahogany chair of Irish Chippendale finely carved. (Courtesy John Bell)

Early Georgian upholstered chairs with straight backs.
Legs in a modified cabriole style. (Courtesy M. Harris)

Two charming early Victorian chairs, either for bedroom or drawing room. Fine carving on the backs.
(Courtesy Silvester)

some to be made, whereupon the gratified workman bestowed on the chair its royal name.

One of the most pleasing chairs which has come down to us is strictly speaking not an antique, as it was produced for Victorian drawing rooms in the early years of Victoria's reign. Extremely dainty and elegant this little chair was made from about 1840 until the latter decades of the century and some were meant for bedroom use, possibly because they were smaller and lighter than most chairs of the time.

In their delicacy of treatment they hint at the kind of chair which Sheraton made for the boudoir. Because of the limited space which they occupy they are still welcome in a bedroom, but they are quite charming in a sitting room today. Indeed they are a welcome addition to a real drawing room as in spite of their delicate appearance they are strong and sturdy. Possessing so many qualities appealing to the modern woman they are quickly increasing in value.

Walnut is the most popular wood employed for this little chair but mahogany with a slight variation of design is also used. The seat is upholstered and is almost rectangular though it widens a little towards the front. The legs are slender and very slightly cabriole and this design, along with the open back, contributes to the air of feminine charm which is so delightful.

The curved back is reeded and sometimes carved in the center. It is built in one piece ascending in flowing lines to the arched top. There is a curved and carved shaped stretcher placed near the actual seat and this links the two sides of the back. The effect of the chair is perhaps too light for dining room use but it is an excellent choice for almost anywhere else in the house.

As has been indicated furniture dating to an earlier period than 1840 is not accepted by the best British Antique Dealers as yet; this in spite of the fact that many Victorian pieces are most desirable. One of these is a mahogany chair made a little later than the walnut chair just dealt with.

It was planned as a bedroom piece in the latter half of the century when suites of furniture were at their height of popularity. It has a smallish square seat, front legs slender and turned, and the back legs square and splaying a little. The open back is square with a solid flat band of mahogany which is often carved, and this forms the top rail. Lower slats and narrow lined slats are attached perpendicularly to the rail until they join a lower rail near the seat which is also turned.

This modest bedroom or sitting room chair can be found without much trouble and while it cannot boast the requisite number of years to make it an antique, it is so ideal for present-day requirements that its sheer usefulness in a little house should be recognized and it must not be rejected out of hand.

There are other small casual chairs, well designed, of walnut or mahogany, which first saw the light during the last century and are worth considering; and as the majority of these are still in excellent condition and could be put to rights by the application of some furniture cream plus some fresh upholstery they may well prove a fine acquisition to the small home.

4

Silver and Sheffield Plate

The origins of many of the items which help to beautify and enrich modern life are so obscure that they are lost in the mists of antiquity. Take for instance glass, silver and gold, as well as mosaics, to name but a few. These were known to the Greeks and the the Egyptians long before the time of Christ, and for several centuries before that the Chinese had acquired the art of producing that exquisite substance which we still call Chinese porcelain.

But not a single name of that select band who plumbed those secrets has come down to us, any more than we have knowledge of the craftsmen who first discovered how to make pewter, nor of him who first made brass.

One name we do know, however. That is the inventor of that delectable metal which we know as Sheffield plate. He was Thomas Bolsover, or Boussover, a Sheffield workman who in 1743 accidentally discovered while working over a fire that silver and copper could be fused together securely at a certain temperature and could be elongated and reduced in thickness by rolling.

He also found that the imposed metals of silver and copper did not split apart in the act of being rolled. Further experiments resulted in the ability to fuse together silver and copper so that the silver appeared on the surface while the copper was con-cealed beneath, thus giving the effect of an article made of sterling silver. Bolsover eventually perfected a sheet of metal which looked like silver but which was welded to a sheet of copper.

Ingenious as this young mechanic was it seems extremely unlikely that he foresaw to any degree the extensive success of his invention, though it must have been obvious from the beginning that it was possible to turn out articles which had all the appearance of genuine silver, at a fraction of the cost of real silver. It should perhaps be added that in very early times the Assyrians had discovered the secret of overlaying iron with bronze, but like other nations who probed into hidden knowledge they kept what they learned to themselves and it did not travel West.

Modestly Bolsover began by manufacturing very small pieces. At that time Sheffield, in addition to being the home of the cutlery trade, also made other articles, including buttons in brass, copper and silver, and Bolsover had the wit to recognize the possibilities which the new metal offered in this field.

This venture was so successful that within a year he was able to return with interest the loan of money which had enabled him to set up in business. He made many small domestic articles such as salt cellars, snuff and patch boxes, buckles, various tiny trinket boxes and caddy spoons often shaped like a shell. He also produced little frivolities for use on dressing tables.

These were quickly succeeded by slightly larger pieces — candle sticks and candelabra, snuffers with matching tray made specially to contain the snuffers. A peep into the early days of the interest in the new plate is given by Horace Walpole who, writing in 1760, a decade or two after the discovery of the new plate, said: "As I went to Lord Stafford's I passed through Sheffield . . . one man there has discovered the art of plating silver with copper. I bought a pair of candlesticks for two guineas which are quite pretty."

Bolsover was not allowed to remain for long the sole manufacturer of the new metal and he was presently joined by Joseph Hancock, another member of the Corporation of Cutlers. Working at the same time, if not quite together, these two men very much increased the type of articles produced, and they turned them out in increasing quantities.

It seems to have been on the initiative of Hancock that they decided to copy the finest and richest embossed silver plate. This was quite an adventure and the list of Sheffield was extended to include tea pots, chocolate pots, cruets, sugars and creams, and trays of all sizes and shapes from little salvers to trays large enough to take the tea service and china. Indeed the output now contained every piece which until then had been made only in genuine silver.

To realize the true value of Bolsover's invention it should be remembered that it came at a time when England was woefully short of silver. In part this was the result of the numerous wars engaged in by the country, when the aristocracy had given much of its silver to be melted down to pay for those expensive operations.

The shortage was also due in part because some of the beautiful ecclesiastical silver had been smuggled abroad at the time when the monasteries were suppressed; and while some of this had been replaced, the aristocracy, who might otherwise have come to the aid of the churches, was so impoverished that they were unable to give much practical help.

For young Bolsover this was a most fortunate state of affairs. It made his products instantly suc-

cessful as so many of his customers were finding that old family silver which had been lost could now be reproduced exactly. This can only be termed good luck. Bolsover's invention was there when it was most needed.

Another happening equally fortunate was the excellence of the designs of existing silver. Had Bolsover made his discovery a hundred years later when the doubtful taste of the Victorians was in full swing, how much poorer would the appearance of the new pieces have been. As it was the importance of the new discovery was quickly appreciated and companies were formed not only in Sheffield but in Birmingham where the mechanics were aided by the more experienced workmen of Sheffield.

Perhaps the greatest attraction of Sheffield plate was not to be discovered for years to come — not only did it look exactly like the genuine articles but it was to retain its silver look over many decades. This was an advantage that could not have been known even to Bolsover. Another interesting point not known was that when, after a period, the copper began to shine through the silver, the value of the piece was not greatly decreased.

It may be stated that all Sheffield plate articles, practically without exception, were reproduced from the sterling article, and therefore any description of a piece of Sheffield may be applied with equal accuracy to a piece of silver. The reverse is not the case. Sheffield plate was not copied by the silversmiths.

Among the smaller, less usual pieces was the tea strainer which like the rest was copied from the genuine silver article. It is interesting to note that the strainer was not at first used for tea, but for straining oranges and lemons, which were a luxury on the English table in the sixteenth century. It is said that lemons were offered at a civic feast given in honor of Henry VIII and Anne Boleyn, and that when James VI and I was king this delicacy was known at that Court also. At that time strainers were also used for some of the coarser wines and for the various possets and herbal drinks in fashion in those days.

The early strainers were purely utility pieces and while they were made of silver they were by no means decorative. A usual design had a tubular handle tapering to a bulging end with a ring terminal convenient for hanging up the strainer when it was not in use. Towards the end of the seventeenth century, however, and coinciding with the growing popularity of tea drinking, strainers found a place among the elegant necessities of the tea table and became much more elaborate.

The design of the bowl became a work of art with piercing in flower head and other motif arrangements and it had on either side flat shaped handles pierced with trefoils and scrolls. And as it was becoming modish to have the owners' initials engraved on spoons and cutlery, some of those were also engraved with piercing so lavish that space for further embellishment was impossible. Sometimes even the maker's name was obliterated.

By the early eighteenth century strainers were made in keeping with the beautiful silver. Circular bowls were often reeded and the piercing carried out in many different patterns with edges that were shaped and gadrooned. The openwork handles, too, were delightfully enriched with chased shells and scrolls. As an indication that the strainer was not used solely for straining tea the interior of the bowl was occasionally shaped like the segments of an orange or a lemon.

The strainer is a rare little object and there are few survivals in Sheffield plate. In the last two decades of the eighteenth century the famous English woman silversmith Hester Bateman designed a strainer whose shape reverted to the earlier type with a tubular handle and a bowl with a reeded rim. This was a favorite finish to much of her silver. As a practical feminine touch she also reintroduced the slender loop handle whereby the strainer might be hung up in the pantry or still-room.

Lemon strainers were made both in silver and in Sheffield plate but they were cast in a more severe mold than the ornate tea strainer, and are not so pleasing in appearance. Cuplike in design the bottom and the sides of the bowl are perforated, and most examples are fitted with two wire handles cut in sufficient length to bridge across the rim of the punch bowl.

Silver punch bowls are attractive pieces to search for. They are rarely found in Sheffield plate as the beverage was going out of favor by the time Sheffield plate was introduced. It is not generally known

that punch originally hailed from India and was made from spirits and water and lemon juice, then sweetened with sugar.

Punch was made in the bowl from which it was served. Its accompaniment was a long-handled ladle which was used to fill the glasses from the bowl. Many old punch bowls were presentation pieces with the engraving still intact and are thus of special interest today; but the plainer bowls are also attractive, and if not used for punch they make charming flower containers.

Punch bowls were frequent products of the nineteenth century and whether made of silver or pottery are most desirable. They are excellent for bulbs and are often acquired for this purpose. In appearance they are circular, very often resting on four small feet; and because they are made of finely designed and colored pottery they are very gay and charming, no matter what their use may be.

It is exciting to come across some of the smaller cupping bowls in silver which were used by sur-

An extremely elegant tureen made in London in 1767 by Thomas Hemming. It has a simple gadroon border and very artistic handles. (Courtesy John Bell)

Beautiful Georgian silver tureen made in London by Phillip Rundell in 1820, the year George IV succeeded to the throne; so the tureen may have been specially made for the coronation. (Courtesy John Bell)

geons and barbers. Very early specimens date to about the first half of the seventeenth century but from about the end of that century they were much more common, and they were made continously throughout the eighteenth century.

Those silver bowls were circular and shallow in shape, and about the time of Queen Anne there might be a fitted cover which along with the bowl was embossed and chased. Towards the end of the century the reeded rim with a circular foot was popular. It was lavishly decorated on the sides with repousee foliage and berries.

For a reason not obvious the Sheffield plate cupping bowls were different in design as instead of being circular they were more often oval and rested on a small foot. Sometimes they were made in pairs but single specimens are more easily found. Key patterns and ring handles with festoon decoration on the covers when those existed made such bowls very elegant.

Sometimes the decoration was quite excessive and is difficult to understand. Chasing and fluting with floral bands and acanthus leaves were fre-

quent, and also surprising as such ornamentation on a piece rarely on show was not often seen.

Small boxes made either of silver or Sheffield plate intended for a variety of uses are fascinating to collect and are still quite numerous. Though originally made to contain such things as snuff, tobacco, medicinal tablets, patches — and a small amount of powder — their size makes them acceptable in a handbag or on a dressing table. Some such little boxes found a new lease on life during the last war when they were used to hold the small ration of sugar, so precious in England at that time.

When produced in silver those boxes were usually of London manufacture but a good proportion of those that were of Sheffield plate were made in Birmingham. These may be quite early as a number were produced just after the discovery of Sheffield plate.

An alluring little piece of Sheffield which is almost a pocket antique is the coaster or decanter stand. This is the kind of piece which can be acquired at random without any worry about matching up different designs, for while those articles which date back to the second half of the eighteenth century were originally turned out in sets of four or six as the correct number for a well-appointed

Small Adam silver bowl made by William Townsend in Dublin about 1770. The decoration is typical of the Adam period and is most delightful. (Courtesy John Bell)

A pair of Scottish eighteenth-century silver entree dishes. Hot water dishes underneath which rest on ball feet.

A graceful Georgian silver basket with swing handle and circular pedestal base. Made in London by Burridge Davenport in 1780. (Courtesy John Bell)

dining table a complete set is rarely found. Designs blend so well with each other that even when bought singly they may be placed close together and still present a harmonious front.

The idea of the coaster is to contain the decanter, and to prevent the polished surface of the table or the lacy tablecloth from being stained by wine which has run down the sides of the bottle. In those convivial days the coaster was an essential article on a gentleman's dining table. Its name incidentally is said to derive from the way the wine coasted round the table after the main dishes of the meal had been removed.

Almost invariably the coaster has a wooden base though an all metal type is not unknown. The wooden bottom however is more practical and is a better protection to the surface of the table which might otherwise be badly scratched by a metal base as it was moved along.

It may be said that almost without exception coasters are extremely beautiful. In actual shape they vary very little. They are circular and are decorated in the conventional fashion of silver designs of the eighteenth century. Some are finished with a wavy beaded edge while others have an unbroken smooth finish, or again the coaster may have a shaped edge ornamented with gadroon touches.

On coasters of a later date, circa the early nineteenth century, the body may be molded and fluted with ornamental gadroon and shell. A delightful

design made in the reign of George III has a rope border and is pierced and chased in an openwork pattern which is delicate and pretty. Another example made about the same time has more discreet ornamentation and has a thread edge and engraved ornament on the sides, with reeding round the base. A fine openwork pattern reappears again at the end of the century and at the beginning of the nineteenth century, and has a rope edge allied to the diamond piercing of the body.

About 1812 a decoration of gadrooning and fluting, which appears on silver teapots and tea services of the day, was repeated on coasters and decanter stands. This most popular design has never quite gone out of fashion, and is found today particularly on teapots, sugars and creams.

Among the small appealing pieces which are tempting to bring home as holiday pieces are snuffers either of silver or of Sheffield plate. Less attractive types of polished steel can sometimes be picked up but they are so rare as to be almost impossible to find. In any case they lack the charm of the finer metals.

Georgian silver teapot made by Charles Fuller of London in 1810. It rests on ball feet and has a pretty handle standing above the pot. (Courtesy John Bell)

Snuffers are now merely ornamental pieces their use having long since gone and they may be hung up on the wall though some specimens are made so that they can stand vertically on a table. A small box which was attached to the snuffers was usually plain though sometimes it was engraved with scrolls.

Into a different category comes the snuffers' tray, which can be put to use in a variety of ways. But in addition this is a piece which is infinitely more artistic than the actual snuffers. Trays in Sheffield are somehow more desirable even than their silver contemporaries though in appearance they appear the same. In shape the tray is oblong but it rarely has straight sides, the long sides being shaped and molded and the short sides rounded.

The outline of the tray is designed to follow the curves of the snuffers which once rested on it and it is typical of the workmanship of the period. Engraving was comparatively frequent but even when the tray was plain it was always well proportioned. Some examples had a small handle fixed on one side and this often had engraving to match that on the main part of the tray and the snuffers. Another supremely attractive design was boat shaped, a popular shape on many silver articles in the eighteenth century.

One of the attractive features of the snuffers' tray is its embellishment. The border is fluted with leaf-like reliefs and as this seldom reveals a join it is suggested that it may have been made in one piece and then attached to the tray. The edges are often reeded or beaded and may be finished with a floral border.

A chased design was frequent and another type of ornament was provided by chased foliage and scrolls, and also the family crest. Some of these old trays achieve a rare loveliness by a combination of fine piercing and delicate chasing, allied to the graceful outline of the tray.

Possibly more in demand by collectors and certainly more easy to come by is the small silver or Sheffield salver or waiter. It should be noted that there is a subtle difference between these two pieces. The oval and oblong shapes are generally accepted as trays, while the small type, square or circular, does not have the importance of that title and is termed a salver.

The salver appeared in England in the latter part of the seventeenth century, possibly about the time of the Restoration when Charles II was bringing so much domestic refinement to the English way of life. At first the salver was used to support such dishes as porringers and tankards, but later servants carried it round when they were offering a glass of wine to a guest. In the early years of the eighteenth century it was referred to as a waiter. Broadly speaking, however, large trays nowadays are "trays" and the smaller ones, whatever their shape, are salvers.

Of the larger trays available a considerable proportion are more often of Sheffield than of silver. Collectors should search for those of oval design with a surrounding pierced gallery, a plain center, and small ball feet as supports. The handles for the tray are formed from spaces in the piercing at each end into which fingers are fitted and the tray lifted. Those trays vary in size. Some are really large while others are quite small.

Beautiful as it is the popularity of the large tray is diminishing for the very practical reason that when it is set out with the cups and other tea things it is so heavy as to be almost impossible to carry from one room to the other.

It is the little salver that every collector longs to

possess, and this whether it be of silver or of Sheffield, and whether it be round or square. The circular shape is most practical when serving glasses of wine or a single cup of tea and it is also very graceful having a subtle grace which is denied to the square type. Some salvers and trays have a surface which is completely plain but fine scrolls, foliage, and crests are often seen.

An interesting point in connection with the applied decoration of trays and salvers is that while other items belonging to the tea equipage were made in suite, this was not done on the trays, whose decoration as it were stood on its own.

In the first part of the eighteenth century silver trays were made in large numbers. This was natural as at that period elegance and beauty were being studied as never before. But as soon as trays were available in the new plate the silver was largely replaced by Sheffield. In the time of Queen Anne the regulation shapes had others added to them. Small octagonal salvers not more than six or seven inches across were exciting novelties.

These small items were sometimes produced in pairs and it is suggested that they might have been used on the dining table possibly for condiments. Sometimes the corners were shaped and fine moldings at the edges made another pleasing finish. From the time of George II deep molded rims were typical. Some examples were ornamented by engraving on the surface and a coat of arms was a frequent decoration.

Others however were quite plain save for borders chased with shells and foliage or there might be a raised pierced border in addition to scrolls and leafy designs. A raised fluted rim and a scalloped edge sometimes appeared and panels of trellis work on a scroll border. Shell engraving which was done circa 1735 was typical of the work of Paul Lamerie, the famous eighteenth-century silversmith.

With the passing of time salvers changed in appearance, not in the actual salver itself but in its supporting feet. The pre-Queen Anne silver types were round and rested on a single stepped central foot with a fairly solid center column, and it looked like a cake dish or a fruit dish. From about the time of the first George the large central support gave way to three or four small ball feet. But the earlier design remained popular and continued in use for several decades, until about the middle of the century.

Drawings of that day seem to indicate that in addition to its use as a tray this mounted salver was sometimes used as a fruit dish to be placed on the sideboard, and it does not seem unlikely that this early salver was the forerunner of the fruit dish as we know it today.

Apart from the matching cream jug and sugar basin there are many pleasing little odd cream jugs quite different in design from the set of teapot, cream and sugar which are amusing to find. When tea was first introduced into England it was served without sugar or cream, in the Oriental fashion, and as no cream receptacles existed which could be copied by the silversmiths, they were modelled on the pewter jugs of the period when they began to be used.

The designs were not particularly good even when reproduced in silver and as the tea drinking custom increased the Queen Anne silversmiths set about designing cream pots more in keeping with the elegant fashions of the period. Among those

An attractive George III cream jug. Reeded on the handle and on the neck. Mounted on a square base. Made by Henry Chawner, the London silversmith, in 1795. (Courtesy John Bell)

were the pear-shaped jug decorated by engravings in rococo style with birds, flowers and fruit, the somewhat top heavy pyriform jug with a handle fashioned like a snake. This rested on a single molded foot. There was also a cast silver cream pot standing on a molded base with a dolphin handle which caused it to be known as the sea monster jug.

The Queen Anne silver tankard was less elaborate but more pleasing in its simplicity. It ranked as successor to the pewter ale jug and it is worth noting that it looked equally as well in silver as it did in pewter, and it was valued sufficiently for it to be preserved as an heirloom.

Gradually the design of the tankard changed and was decorated with gadrooning and fluting. Other jugs which followed the pewter shapes had bulbous bodies on molded bases, and they had graceful

A most pleasing Georgian tankard, baluster shaped, made by the famous eighteenth-century London silversmith Hester Bateman in 1781. The lid has a beautifully pierced thumb piece and is exquisitely designed. (Courtesy John Bell)

scroll handles, often scrolled, and wide lips.

Also included in the small coterie of desirable little pieces are sugar casters. They were originally made in sets of three, one for sugar, one for pepper, and one for spice. The latter type were termed muffineers and were used for sprinkling spice on toasted muffins.

Casters date from the time of William and Mary and early examples were shaped like a column with a flat blind top; and they rested on a reeded molded base slightly stepped. The pierced holes to release the sugar were fitted about a third of the way down the caster. Scroll decoration was sometimes found on the body of the piece.

Queen Anne's reign saw a more elaborate design with straight sides and mushroom-shaped domes which were perforated in concentric circles. In some dredgers the body was vase-shaped with a bulge immediately above the short-stepped stem and there was usually a small knop on the cap, shaped like a cone or acorn. Most casters are finished with the same type of foot, a circular base, reeded or stepped, which provided both a solid support and gave a certain dignity to the caster.

Another caster made about the same time can best be described by likening it to the old fashioned pepper pot which was used in the kitchen then and throughout the years since that time. It had straight sides extending slightly at the base, a pierced mushroom top, and a plain but graceful handle.

The daintiness of the caster as a dining table piece lent itself to a considerable variation in decoration. Floral chasing with foliage, gadroon borders, reeded borders, ornamental caps and fine piercing, were all present in different degrees, and latterly an elongated cap gave a fresh importance to so small a piece. While casters were copied in Sheffield plate these are less plentiful than the silver examples.

Collectors will not ignore the charms of the little sweetmeat dish one of the daintiest productions of the eighteenth century. It is rather surprising that taking into account the scarcity and cost of sugar at that time, there could not have been a great variety in the choice of available sweetmeats, that those small containers should have been made at all.

Lovely eighteenth-century chocolate pot with high lid and finial. Ivory handle and delightful decoration.

Four William III trencher salts, with bold gadrooning. (Courtesy Asprey)

They had actually appeared though in smaller numbers in the first part of the seventeenth century when the design was circular, small, beaded at the edges, embossed with fruit, and fitted with a handle. In Queen Anne's time the dishes were still small and shallow and were fitted with a flat swing handle and sometimes there was fluting and also an escalloped border.

Later in the century the oval sweetmeat dish was popular. It was a most elegant acquisition to the dining table, as it was pierced and chased with embossed sides, beaded borders, and it too had a swing handle.

Perhaps the most charming sweetmeat dish is fashioned like a miniature cake basket with fluting and gadrooning and having a bail handle. It was also made in Sheffield plate and may have a lining of blue glass. This was an unusual feature as glass linings were not usually added to sweetmeat dishes.

Much of the beauty of early eighteenth century silver and that of the sister metal, Sheffield plate, owes a great deal to the Huguenot silversmiths who had to flee their country at the Revocation of the Edict of Nantes, in 1685, by Louis XIV. Their skilled continental workers greatly aided the English craftsmen by bringing new ideas across the Channel.

Coming at the time of the increased prosperity of the middle classes this created a market for their goods and at the same time encouraged buyers to improve their stocks. The renaissance of art in England during the latter years of the seventeenth century as applied to the production and decoration of domestic articles was due in no small measure to the taste and skill of those Huguenots.

One of the Huguenots of that era was Paul de Lamerie who as an infant was brought by his parents to Britain in 1689, and who was to find fame in his adopted country as its premier goldsmith and silversmith.

The Lameries were of aristocratic descent and it was because of their Protestant faith that they were driven from their country. As an impoverished aristocrat Paul de Lamerie senior had not been brought up to learn any trade, and life for the younger Paul was very hard indeed. When he was about fifteen he was apprenticed to Peter Platel a skillful silversmith and also a Protestant of gentle birth. Platel was to become de Lamerie's father-in-law.

By 1712 young Paul de Lamerie was admitted a Freeman of the city "by servitude through the Goldsmiths' company," and set up his own business near the "Hay Markett." It was obvious from the first that he was a great artist but there was also a practical side to his character. In this he resembled Robert Adam who not only designed houses for his clients but in addition advised them on interior decoration, and planned for them the kind of furniture which would blend best with his architecture.

De Lamerie was not content to create beautiful pieces of silver but when the order was being delivered to his customers he enclosed directions as to the care and cleaning of the silver and general preservation. His skill and workmanship were quickly recognized not only in England but in other countries as well, and from 1712 until 1751 when he died he was the greatest English exponent of his art.

While still a young man, in his thirties, he was commissioned to do work for the Russian Court and later he produced some fine chandeliers for the Kremlin. In spite of this, however, a large proportion of his work was domestic silver, and he designed many of the beautiful tea services which were coming into fashion and his tea and coffee pots were notable expressions of his genius. Elegant sugars and creams, cake baskets, salvers and sweetmeat dishes were all grist to the mill.

Lamerie was aided by the adventurous spirit of the times when the great merchant ships were voyaging farther than ever before and were beginning to trade with newly discovered nations, and were bringing back to England new merchandise and new methods of working.

At the start of his working career de Lamerie's models were simple in design but from these he passed to others which were more decorative but never ultra ornate. Even in his later years when his pieces showed richly chased rococo ornament and almost extravagant embellishment the effect was still superb. He is the best known of the early English silversmiths and all others must take a lower place.

But another famous London silversmith of an earlier date was George Heriot of Trabourn in

Haddingtonshire, son of an Edinburgh silversmith of repute. He was born in 1563. His workmanship was much valued in Scotland and it was due to the interest of James I of the United Kingdom that he was appointed Court jeweller and moved south with the Court to London. He succeeded so well that in later years when the king was in financial difficulties Heriot came to the royal rescue.

Another famous craftsman who was working in London at a slightly earlier period was Sir Thomas Greshman who was born in 1519 and who was elected Lord Mayor of London. He too was very successful and one of his early transactions was to supply a "cheyne of fine golde" to the fourth wife of Henry VIII, Anne of Cleaves. He was better known for his Courtly connections, it is said, than for the excellence of his workmanship.

5

Victoriana

Successful furnishing is never easy. This is a statement which applies particularly to furnishing in antique, and it is fascinating to study just how the happiest interiors have achieved their harmony and grace. Surprisingly this effect often arrives by a gradual accumulation of one purchase following another with no clear picture of the future in the mind of the owner.

This happened possibly more frequently than a conscious desire to fill the home with select pieces of Chippendale, Hepplewhite, or Sheraton. The possession of one very good piece leads to another, and when one thinks of a house or flat which one specially admires it is obvious that its beauty seems to be the result of careful planning. There has actually been little discrimination beyond the purchaser's taste.

Naturally, care must have been taken in the choice of chairs, tables and the like; colors will be in harmony, a piece of tapestry here, gay flags of cushions there. So much beauty could not be accidental. It must all have been selected piece by piece.

But this is only part of the truth. Furnishing is not simply a form of buying. Even in this workaday world there are still such excitements as legacies and gifts of furniture. Some are eminently suitable for their new surroundings, some are not.

But it is extraordinary that in time they seem to settle down and blend with the furniture which is already there. And over the years when colors fade in wood as well as in wool, the room gradually takes on that planned appearance.

There is no background more pleasing than a room which looks as if it had acquired this intentionally; a beautiful home which in part at least has achieved this beauty accidentally. There is the other side of furnishing, however, when the owners do not know what they want in their homes and work very hard to obtain it — sometimes successfully, sometimes less so.

At this stage it should perhaps be said that there is such a thing as too much respect for period. Period is important, but it may be added that it follows good taste. And this never keeps company with overcrowding.

Another point worth noting is that in the eighteenth century and during a good part of the nineteenth the majority of well-to-do families settled themselves in a house which seemed likely to supply their needs for some time to come. In many cases they remained there for the greater part of their lives and so when they chose furniture and furnishings they did so in the knowledge that this was likely to be their permanent home.

At that time there was more furniture to choose

from, more pieces in more colors than had ever been the case before, and by the end of the reign of George IV, about 1830, a new phrase was introduced into the general speech of the furnishing world. This was rococo. It was a vernacular term usually applied to taste, which had been borrowed from France, where, according to Ralph Edwards, it was used to describe disparingly "any fashion in decoration, dress or manners regarded as antiquated, freakish or affected."

Some authorities trace its origin to the elaborate grottoes with which Catherine de Medici, an Italian who married Henry II of France in 1533, decorated the gardens of Les Tuilleries. When these were made they were called rocailleurs in France.

Rococo was expressed only by surface ornament and when fashion decreed that it should take the form of applied mounts and gilded bronze on chests, chairs, and tables there was a tendency for it to overwhelm the object which it was meant to adorn by the glitter of its richness of style. But with other pieces, including console tables and chandeliers, mirrors, clock cases and candle stands, an admirable result was achieved.

Although it had been known in France for centuries it fell out of favor in that country in the nineteenth century, because it somehow suggested a lack of breeding and did not tone in with the general furnishing schemes. It reached England a short time before Victoria came to the throne in 1837, and when it was used on English chairs, chests and tables its rather fanciful style did not seem to harmonize with the mode there.

Neither was it suited to the capacities of the English cabinet makers, and though it was bought and sold to an extent that it was considered a part of the English furniture scene during the early part of last century the part it played was small. It is not really typical of the kind of furniture now referred to as Victorian.

There are almost certainly more Victorian antiques to be had at the moment than of any other period, though in a sense this is a contradiction in terms, as the best antique dealers in the United Kingdom reject a piece of furniture as antique if it was not made before 1830, and it is not included in that category of antique goods they have for sale.

As many beautiful pieces were turned out about 1840 or 1850 it should be added that this ruling, while it prevails in London and in some of the larger cities of Britain, is not accepted entirely by collectors. A discriminating buyer may well find something belonging to the Victorian era very worthwhile acquiring. Also, furniture periods blend closely with each other and a table which appears to be, say, Regency may actually have been made by a Victorian craftsman copying an earlier design.

It is generally admitted that by the time Victorian pieces came on the market they were suffering from the malaise of taste that had deteriorated, and a knowledgeable collector may have a dislike for the "busyness" of a good deal of their designs — the addition of superlative carving, the unnecessary bits and pieces that appeared on wardrobes and beds for no special reason, and the enbonpoint which added to the suggestion of bulk on a sideboard.

After the restrained good taste of the eighteenth century there was suddenly a range of furniture which had a little too much of everything. There were ornaments galore, over decorated cushions, bubble trimming on curtains till it became an interference, lavishly carved legs on dining tables. In moderation it would have been excellent, and to the Victorians it seemed excellent for a very long time, practically until the end of the century.

At the same time one cannot deny that there are many delightful Victorian pieces which are worth searching for and it is up to the discerning collector to pick these out. Already in the past few years these have soared a good deal in price.

Among the more attractive pieces are the small Victorian armchairs which were originally upholstered in plush or velvet, button backed, and having a carved frame of mahogany or rosewood. These are in great demand at present especially among young marrieds who cover them in a matt material such as repp in a strong gay color, pillar box red or a vivid green, or even orange which does not look amiss if the background is right. This is a good casual chair for a bedroom as it has a certain amount of comfort and does not take up too much room.

Very desirable is the early Victorian chiffonier. This piece with the French name had already appeared during the Regency era as a suitable candidate for the parlor which was then just coming into fashion. Its usefulness, its modest appearance, and the fine workmanship all combined to assure its popularity. The earlier chiffonier was made of rosewood, the accepted wood of the time, but the Victorian specimens are of mahogany.

While there is one basic design for the chiffonier it varies in detail. The lower half resembles a sideboard in that there is a long drawer — sometimes two — beneath the top of the main part, and underneath there are panelled cupboards made to contain the same kind of necessities as the sideboard does.

The arrival of the chiffonier on the domestic scene was the direct result of changing conditions.

One of these was the displacement of the large house with numerous apartments which were not essential. The new type of house was of a much more manageable size with rooms that were fewer in number and smaller in cubic space. This necessitated smaller furniture being made to fit these rooms.

It was because of this that the parlor came into being, a room which was not quite a dining room and not quite a sitting room. It was furnished with a smallish dining table and a couple of easy chairs as well as the usual chairs used for meals, and it became the right thing for the middle classes to have their meals in the parlor during the week, and dine in stately splendor in the dining room proper

Unusual eighteenth-century mahogany Pembroke table with finely shaped top center drawer with shaped front; square tapered legs with a touch of inlay. (Courtesy Charles Lumb)

at the week-end when the family was probably augmented by visitors. The parlor was a friendly room and it was used for sitting in when the members of the family were alone. As a fashion it was a great success.

For a present-day collector the furnishings from a Victorian parlor form a mine of possibilities and from such beginnings there may stem the nucleus of the kind of dining room we have today: a room partly to eat in and partly to sit in, with adjustments on both counts.

There is not a dining table in the parlor, as the word used to be understood, but one which can be folded to suit smaller surroundings. Among the best of these is the Pembroke table. Not too cumbersome, not too small, with a large enough top when this is extended, and with folding hinged leaves at the "long sides" which transform it into a big enough board to seat in comfort six or eight guests. It also contains a fairly roomy drawer which in a little room is a godsend for holding cutlery.

Pembroke tables can still be picked up without much trouble. Mahogany is the wood used most frequently but as it was a Regency piece it is also found in rosewood. The most desirable examples have straight tapered legs but others with turned legs which were produced later in the reign should not be despised.

The Pembroke is a modest table with rarely any decoration but some of the Sheraton specimens show a touch of inlay on the drawer, the flaps may have reeded edges, and very occasionally the flaps are made in ovals instead of being rectangular. This latter feature is a delightful change when the table is either closed or open and adds considerably to the appearance of the table. It was planned as an every day parlor piece but today when the dining room is so limited in space its desirability can scarcely be exaggerated.

Any one who lives alone should not ignore the small circular table made of two half moon ends which once formed the two ends of a large dining table. As has been mentioned in another chapter two semi circular halves placed together make an ideal small dining table. These are most often found in mahogany and it is surprising how many such tables have survived from the Victorian era.

One of the most eminent pieces of Victoriana is the sofa table. This is an eighteenth-century table but it continued to be made during last century. It is quite an enchanting table either for eating from or as a dressing table. Its name arose from the fact that women of the eighteenth century who were inveterate letter writers developed the curious, and one would imagine the uncomfortable, habit of conducting their correspondence from the sofa table. It was long and very narrow in proportion, with hinged flaps at either end which could be raised to extend the length still further and in this fashion it was an imposing piece.

Authorities do not always agree on the originator of the sofa table but if Sheraton did not actually introduce it he must have made some of the first examples, for the convenience of the letter writers of the day. Sofa tables can be dated in part by the kind of wood which was used in their manufacture. Early specimens were usually in mahogany with discreet inlay accompanied by cross bandings of ebony and sometimes by a hint of satinwood which Sheraton used most lavishly.

In Regency tables the popular wood was rosewood and that was used in place of mahogany, but by the early decades of the nineteenth century, taste was not so reliable as it had been and every bit of furniture, including sofa tables, suffered accordingly.

It may be of interest to collectors to note that the larger sofa tables are the most pleasing and are the kind to look for. The large table continued to be produced throughout the greater part of Victoria's reign, but some smaller ones appeared in the latter decades of the nineteenth century, and at the beginning of this century also, and these are much less appealing.

Among the surplus type of furniture one often finds some desirable pieces. A whatnot for instance can be a delightful possession though as its name suggests it seems to have had a vague beginning. It appeared a short time before the time of Victoriana and was know in many of the Regency drawing rooms before it made a niche for itself in the Victorian background.

It is a pity that the resourceful cabinet makers of the time did not discover a more elegant name for this collection of three or four trays joined at the corners by small turned supports and resting on four little feet. Walnut was a favorite wood for the whatnot, rosewood was used in the Regency period, and in the later examples mahogany appeared.

Invariably the design was simple, the trays being either square or rectangular with no applied decoration. Sometimes there was a low brass gallery fitted to the topmost tray and occasionally there was a little gallery also on the other trays.

Legs on whatnots are usually slender and are turned, sometimes twisted, like barley sugar, and are fitted with casters so that the piece is easily moved about. This makes it an adaptable asset either in a drawing room or in a dining room where it can act successfully as a trolley and when not required for this purpose it can be placed against a wall to hold decorative little pieces of china or glass.

Nowadays it is often used in a small dining room as an aide to serving plates or food, but it is also desirable as a fireside piece or as a convenient repository for books and magazines. Where no actual dining room exists and space is restricted it is a suitable table for the radio, for cold dishes brought in from the kitchen, and when it is fitted with a little shallow drawer at the base, as it occasionally is, this can take some of the cutlery, and some of the smaller appointments.

A whatnot is a pleasing and useful acquisition

Whatnot with very slender supports and an inlaid drawer. (Courtesy John Bell)

and makes an attractive background for little articles which otherwise do not have a permanent home. Perhaps the most pleasing type is the walnut whatnot in a lovely faded golden brown color and having some inlay edging the trays. It is still quite easy to find and is not too expensive, though in recent years it has risen in price; and in common with other attractive Victoriana the cost is still rising.

Victorian toilet mirrors are pleasing little pieces. They do not belong to the category of the exquisite dressing glasses made during the eighteenth century but with some searching it is possible to find one of good proportions. There is a general impression that all such glasses belonging to the Victorian era are well made but clumsy and badly designed and not really desirable.

This is by no means accurate though if possible it is advisable to place a Victorian toilet glass in company with other pieces of approximately the same period.

The skeleton design can be most pleasing, that is, a mirror which is swung between two side supports which at this period are usually turned; it has a shaped stretcher beneath but no drawers or other fitment. The Victorian skeleton mirror lacks the grace of its earlier sisters but it is still reminiscent of the fine eighteenth-century skeleton glasses, and it is infinitely superior to those mirrors produced later in the reign, when thicker lines blurred the clarity of design without adding anything pleasing in its place.

The frame of the Victorian skeleton glass is usually rectangular and the appearance is improved when this is not too broad. There is indeed a skeleton glass with a large mirror and a very narrow frame made fairly early in the reign, which has narrow supports and stretchers, and this can be a most pleasing piece. Most of the small mirrors made about that time are of mahogany.

One of the most delectable pieces turned out in Victoria's reign is the little walnut drawing room table. Without reserve this can be a most pleasing addition to a sitting room. It may be circular with a mushroom-shaped top but less frequent and more attractive is the oval top. This is mounted on a single turned and carved leg which broadens slightly as it falls downwards. It then breaks away into a pedestal of three curved, carved legs which are slightly splayed.

The table is finished with an unusual finial falling almost to the floor between the legs. Its shape is rather like a flattened knop with a much smaller knop beneath it. While this is definitely a Victorian piece it bears evidence of Sheraton influence in the top which very often has a center of inlay done in different colored woods in quiet tones. There may also be an edging of ebony which throws the golden color of the walnut into relief.

Another pleasing little piece, and one which is already regaining some of the popularity it had a hundred years ago, is the small circular foot stool. When they were originally made those stools appeared in pairs but in the course of time they have become odd pieces surviving mostly as single items. The industrious women of that age covered them in tapestry which was often further ornamented by beadwork in blended shades.

This made for an attractive little stool but as they had to combat a constant rubbing from the slippers which rested on them, the colors of the wool gradually became dull and lost their brightness. A heavy wine color or dull green were favorite colors for the wools — also surprisingly a dark shade of brown was favored for the background.

Now and again, however, a stool emerges which was first embroidered in a really bright color with beadwork in colors equally strong, and such a stool if it has been cared for may still retain its original colors with unexpected charm.

The Victorian stool is a workmanlike little piece. It was not intended to be an ornament but as a means of resting tired feet. The center of tapestry is joined to a narrow circle of mahogany or rosewood, and it is finished by three small feet — sometimes four — emerging at the base. These somehow give the stool a certain importance, and remove it from the category of being just a little stool without feet.

In the mid-Victorian years a higher stool, which seems to have been planned as an extra seat, was produced. It was not so high as a chair but higher than the majority of contemporary stools and it appears likely that it was intended as a fireside seat.

This stool was square and had four turned knopped legs which were usually of mahogany but quite frequently were of walnut; and less attractive types might be of rosewood or of some of the fruit woods. Surrounding the upholstered top was a support about three inches deep of matching wood. This was covered in velvet of a color to match the tapestry top and was trimmed with galon. Any collector who is anxious to cover a stool like this should endeavor to find a piece of old silk velvet which has so much more grace than modern velvet.

Sometimes a heavy plush or velvet was used for the upholstery on those stools and this was edged with a fringe about three inches deep which hung over and partially covered the side pieces of wood. But the velvet is not so thrifty a covering as tapestry or a stronger furnishing material. As in the case of the very small round stool beadwork was a usual decoration. This was most effective especially when carried out to tone with the background wool embroidery.

Those stools dated approximately to the middle years of Victoria's reign when colors were more gay than in the later decades and it is noteworthy that the general effect of the stool being bright, the best wood for it was walnut. Darker woods such as mahogany and rosewood and birch seem to detract from the general appearance of the brightly embroidered stool.

About 1860 the Victorians produced a stool which is so pleasing both in design and effect that it can be compared with those of any other age, without fear that it might clash with its companions. This stool stands fairly high and is rectangular in shape but the lower part of the frame was sometimes serpentine and was finished with small brass nails, a kind of throwback to the early years of the eighteenth century — but very attractive.

In the early years of Victoria's reign some alluring little dressing tables appeared. They were not part of a bedroom suite but were individual pieces, and they resembled the kind of tables made by Sheraton, keeping the good features of that period without acquiring any of the less agreeable tendencies. They were probably made first of all, circa 1810, by country workmen who still followed the old fashions, and they continued to be made in rural areas for several decades afterwards.

Mahogany was the wood most frequently used with occasional changes to rosewood, the Regency

A fine Sheraton painted and inlaid satinwood secretaire or chiffonier with decorated cupboards beneath. (Courtesy Gregory & Co.)

favorite. The design followed that of a flat-topped writing desk with three top drawers, one in the center and two at each side, and a kneehole fixed beneath the center drawer. The legs were graceful and slender and nicely turned. Sometimes the kneehole space was halfmoon in shape, sometimes only slightly curved, or it might be straight following the line of the drawer above.

In the earlier specimens the drawer handles were small and round and made of brass, but in the later **examples the bail handle ceased and instead of a brass handle there was a small circular wooden knob.** This was a really small piece, perhaps about thirty-six inches long, and therefore a most acceptable piece for present-day usage in a small room.

Few pieces are more typical of the Victorian era than the chiffonier. As has been said, it was built on the same lines as a sideboard but on a much reduced scale. It has shelved cupboards in the lower part fitted behind panelled doors, or behind doors that are almost plain, while above there are one or two longish shallow drawers. Above this there is a flat top which may or may not have a small enclosed cupboard fixed at the back and there may be a decoration of finely latticed brass fitted at each end, in the form of a low gallery. This feature is reminiscent of Sheraton who liked decorating his sideboards in this fashion.

In later chiffoniers a permanent straight mirror was fixed between the two small cupboards but in the earlier pieces this Victorian characteristic was lacking. In design the mid-nineteenth century chiffonier had a higher waist than that found on the sideboards of the time, and as it was much shorter in length it gave the impression of being somewhat squat. At the same time its proportions are good, and it is easily placed in a modern apartment.

Though the chiffonier occasionally has small feet it more often stands on the main part of the piece. Very much like it is the Regency type which is usually referred to as a cabinet. It also has the panelled cupboards in the lower part and the shallow horizontal drawers, and it has small carved feet back and front.

There is a difference in the top, however. The little square cupboards are missing, there is not a glass mirror, and the back is high with a shaped support and a shelf which extends the length of the cabinet. Books and china were sometimes kept in those Regency cabinets. Rosewood was commonly used though mahogany was not unknown.

The Regency cabinet is not easy to find but there are still a good many chiffoniers of the Victorian era on the market. Those in good condition have appreciated very much in value of recent years. Mahogany which was the most popular wood in Victorian times is more frequent than rosewood but both woods are still to be found.

A most graceful early Victorian acquisition is the small bookcase which first appeared during the Regency period but remained in fashion for many decades. Of good proportions it consists of a shelved interior usually of mahogany or rosewood, protected by two glazed doors. There are touches of inlay and slender columns are fitted at each end of the piece. A rather delightful note of decoration is provided by a narrow brass gallery which borders the top.

Pretty early Victorian miniature bureau and bookcase. Made in rosewood. Tapered legs and spade feet and cross stretchers. Fitted with a drawer which is serpentine shaped. (Courtesy John Bell)

Usually the bookcase has no feet and rests solidly on the floor. A practical touch is the varied spacing between the shelves. This is deep and thus allows for high upstanding books. This piece can also be used most happily as a china cupboard. It is characteristic of the Regency period when the furniture was transitory and did not show any particular individuality, save that it was partly a reflection of the French Empire styles introduced at the close of the Terror years in the last decade of the eighteenth century.

At that time Victorian ideas were beginning to cast their shadow but the good designs that had been in vogue for so long had not yet gone. Unfortunately there was no new race of skilled designers waiting to mold public taste and create fresh beauty from wood. Regency styles while not notably aesthetic had one commendable feature: they were planned to suit the smaller homes which were being put up, and the furniture was most usable, produced for ordinary people and eminently suitable for the age.

During the Victorian-Regency era small open bookcases were often produced in pairs and this proved an imagiative design. To begin with, while they are not joined to it, they were used along with a chiffonier — a bookcase at each end. This idea was most successful, as the proportions were neat and the piece adaptable.

Later, those bookcases became fireside pieces which was perhaps their most delightful use. They were narrow and not very high, and therefore took up very little space. A shallow drawer carved or inlaid was sometimes fitted to the top, and slender turned columns at either end of the bookcase added a pleasing note of ornamentation.

Some of the early Victorian bookcases rest on small bun feet and are fitted with several graded shelves with the smallest shelves at the top. This bookcase is usually found in mahogany with the supporting sides delicately shaped.

In the search for Victoriana small chairs should not be overlooked. Some specimens are quite small and were originally intended for drawing-room use when they helped to eke out the existing seating accommodation. The most desirable type is very reminiscent of Sheraton. It was made of walnut and had an open curved and carved back with slats sometimes, which stretched across the back. The front legs were most decorative. They were very slightly cabriole with small paw feet and were sometimes reeded. The back legs were plain and splayed a little. Though those chairs were sometimes used in bedrooms they were not really bedroom pieces.

The Victorians covered the upholstered tops of such chairs with material to match the curtains of the room, preferably in not too bright a color. Brocade had a certain popularity and there was a vogue for a dull satin material, while for a country cottage, chintzes in clear colors were in demand, but any good design will blend with those chairs, provided the colors are clear.

In the middle years of the Victorian reign those extremely dainty chairs were replaced by others, which though they had not the same charm of the early specimens were still pleasing. The legs were turned and slender and the backs were still open but they were square rather than curved and slatted horizontally as well as perpendicularly. One notable difference was that they were not made in walnut but in mahogany.

Those chairs were usually made for bedroom use and they remained in fashion until the end of the reign and beyond it. They can be picked up without too much trouble; they are easy to place either in a hall or in a room, as they blend quite well with modern styles. Also they have not yet soared in price as the little walnut chairs have done.

Small hanging shelves made either of mahogany or rosewood are so eminently attractive in a little room that if they had not been introduced in an earlier period, someone must surely have discovered their usefulness today. They are the answer to a definite need for a small piece, which will take either china or books, in many small homes where a piece like this is much required.

One of the greatest advantages of those hanging shelves is that as they are suspended on the wall they take up no space in a room which might be required for something else, and in spite of their small size they can accommodate an astonishingly large number of books or small ornaments. They are also quite decorative though the design is simple. The piece consists of three shelves held together by narrow turned supports which pierce the corners at each end which are otherwise exposed.

Set of Sheraton hanging bookshelves in mahogany.
(Courtesy John Bell)

Small mahogany desk, shaped front turned legs and
small gallery round the top. (Courtesy John Bell)

Some authorities give Chippendale the credit for the introduction of the set of hanging shelves and he certainly produced some delightful designs with latticed sides and a small latticed feature at the top on each side. Occasionally, too, there was a very shallow drawer fixed to the base of the shelves; or there might be two little drawers.

The Chippendale shelves were usually in mahogany as were those made by Hepplewhite. The hanging shelves turned out by Hepplewhite were less attractive than Chippendale's type and less attractive too than the unpretentious Victorian specimens. Where Chippendale had latticed sides the Hepplewhite design was apt to be solid and as they had shaped fronts this did not add to their general charm.

It is not often that a Victorian piece can match up in attraction with others made in the eighteenth century but the small hanging shelves of the nineteenth century are pleasant little pieces, with little ornamentation save a small brass gallery which sometimes adorns the top. Occasionally the shelves were linked together at the corners by columns of brass instead of wood, and there might be a delicate finial above the columns.

An increasing amount of reading was done in the eighteenth century but it was in the nineteenth century, by which time books were much cheaper, that it was at its height. Education too had spread widely and consequently the numbers of readers had multiplied. Leaving aside the question of displaying pieces of fine china and porcelain, which was very fashionable, the vogue for so many hanging shelves is a proof of the love of reading which permeated all classes in England in the last century.

A small desk peculiarly suited to the needs of our present day was produced in the early Victorian era. This was called a davenport. It was much in demand throughout the nineteenth century and after a spell of not being appreciated it is now enjoying a fresh surge of popularity, as it is small enough to live happily in a modest sitting room and yet big enough to perform the function for which it was designed.

Designed like a bureau with a sloping lid the hinged top slopes downwards towards the front, and stretches far enough forward to provide a kind of kneehole for the comfort of the writer. When the desk is opened one can see that the back is fitted with several small writing compartments though these do not have the same fine finish nor the extent of detail of eighteenth-century bureaux.

At each side of the main part of the desk there is a perpendicular row of three or four shallow drawers, and these drawers reach to the floor. On one side the drawers are sham so they only operate from the side which can be drawn out, and were presumably made like this so as to give balance to the piece. The drawers are deep enough to contain an adequate amount of stationery and writing materials.

The drawers have small circular wooden knobs as handles, and on some of the davenports, though not on them all, there may be locks and keys. In some specimens a tiny drawer is fitted above the tier of drawers and it also is opened from the outside. It is small, narrow, with very little depth, and just large enough to take pens and oddmenta of correspondence.

The davenport is characteristically Victorian, and is usually made of mahogany though some examples are of rosewood. It is strong and sturdy like all the Victorian pieces of excellent workmanship so that in spite of its size it cannot be readily knocked over. It lacks too the superfluity of decoration which was common in much of the furniture of the period and it has a pleasing appearance.

There is carving sometimes on the lower part of the davenport, just beneath the sloping front. There are no legs attached to this piece. It rests squarely on the ground and while not unduly elegant it presents quite an attractive appearance.

In addition to the usual woods — mahogany and rosewood — of which the davenport was composed it was also made occasionally of the fruit woods and of birch. Only rarely was it produced in walnut. It

Small Sheraton desk decorated with touches of inlay. Straight legs. (Courtesy John Bell)

Davenport with sloping top. Mahogany. (Courtesy Silvester of Solihull)

is a commendable piece of work turned out by the Victorian craftsmen.

The introduction of the desk was an indication as to how the cabinet makers of the Victorian period sought to please their feminine clientele. It was one of the few really feminine pieces which had been turned out since the early eighteenth century craftsmen began to take their needs and desires into account. It must have been a joy to Victorian womanhood.

6

Pottery and Porcelain

Of the smaller antiques one of the most colorful is old English pottery. Its inception is usually credited to the workers of the eighteenth century, but one of the best modellers whose name has come down to us was John Dwight of Fulham who was born in 1637 and who died in 1703.

Dwight produced figures and busts. The figures were usually mythological characters while the busts represented royal personages, such as Charles II and his Queen, James II and Prince Rupert. For a time those pieces were a triumphant success but specimens of Dwight's work are not likely to be found nowadays outside museums.

In the last decade of the seventeenth century the Elers brothers began manufacturing, in England, a new red earthenware expressed in small ornaments and figures, and surprisingly enough in teapots, all made in colored clays. About this time the English potters were trying to imitate the white Oriental china of the East, and salt ware was made from about the end of the seventeenth century until 1780.

Potteries began to extend, notably in Staffordshire, in what came to be known as the pottery towns. Their first figures made in delft glazed stone were primitive with a limited range of colors, but by the middle of the century potters were less amateurish and more venturesome and small fig-

ures in colored clays were tinted all over with a lead glaze. Those were very tiny, only a few inches high, and the favorite subjects were toy soldiers, equestrians and bandsmen — a Catholic choice.

The early colors though few were bold and effective — yellow, pale blue, green, rust, and several shades of brown, but never vermillion or crimson. But the potters worked on those colors until almost any other color could be reproduced. When they learned how to add red, that in particular added greatly to the gay effect.

The best known of all the potters, Josiah Wedgwood, was apprenticed to his brother Thomas in 1744 when he was only fourteen. He was still a young man when he succeeded in producing a green glaze for covering dessert plates; and dishes decorated with leaves and fruit and specimens of those green plates, while not plentiful, can still be had.

He also turned out lids for vegetable dishes made in the form of a vegetable, such as cauliflower, and in 1762 he made his famous cream ware which was sometimes called Queen's ware because it was popular with the royal house. This ware was in such demand that it ousted the salt glaze ware. Wedgwood was one of the first of the potters to mark his pieces.

Early potters copied each other's work to a considerable extent, including Josiah Wedgwood himself, but it is also true that ideas for the first pottery produced in England were taken from the Chinese pieces which trading merchants were bringing back in increasing numbers, such as tea and coffee sets in imitation of Chinese red porcelain.

It is interesting to compare the difference between various pieces of porcelain; and these are not only chemical differences but textile; that is to say in the feel and touch. Porcelain is a fine stone ware, a cold fabric which can be worked in great detail while pottery is coarser and more crude both in conception and appearance. But pottery possesses an element of warmth, difficult to describe but very appealing. Porcelain is the aristocrat of the two.

Though all sorts of articles were modelled in potttery, including jugs, mugs, cups, money boxes, tea and coffee pots as well as posset pots, the most popular were the figures, either single or in groups. There was also a great demand for animals such as dogs, cats, monkeys, and cocks and hens.

From the beginning of the nineteenth century it was modish to reproduce celebrities such as famous divines like the Wesley brothers, and George Whitfield; and national heroes like Nelson, Wellington, and the Prince Consort were commemorated in pottery. The Wesleys were friends of Ralph and Enoch Wood, the well-known Burslem potters, and the bust of John Wesley was done by Enoch when he was a guest of the Woods and was staying with them, while he was preaching in Staffordshire. At that time the youthful potter was in his early twenties, while Wesley was about eighty-eight. It is said that the workmanship of this particular piece was so fine that it made Wedgwood's name as a pottery sculptor.

Towards the end of the eighteenth century, and afterwards, pottery figures tended to be sporting or merely decorative. There were shepherds and shepherdesses, huntsmen and gamekeepers, usually modelled in their workaday clothes, and as such figures were familiar to the country folk with whom they found a ready sale, they were carried around in pedlar's packs and proved more popular than busts of royalties and celebrities.

Many beautiful jugs were turned out by all the best-known Staffordshire potters. In the first quarer of the nineteenth century there was a vogue for

An unusual pair of Staffordshire figures representing two children riding on goats. (Courtesy John Bell)

Small porcelain figure of a cat. Decorative for a country cottage. (Courtesy John Bell)

ordering jugs of a special design with the initials of the owner and the date of purchase painted on it. Those jugs were quite delightful painted in the most exquisite shades often having delicate floral patterns. They were made in various sizes and sometimes there was an unsusual feature showing the handle emerging from the inside of the jug body and then finishing up in the normal place. Those jugs were cherished possessions.

Many ornamental pottery center pieces were produced in Leeds ware but the chief specialties of the factory there were dessert, tea and dinner services where there was the unusual feature of perforated covers. These were found on sugar bowls and soup tureens and on trays, and this typical decoration appeared also on cruet stands, flower vases, and as an upstanding edge around the lid of a teapot.

A very fine cream ware for domestic use was one of the products of the Leeds factory. Its chief characteristics were a trellis of open-work bordering the plates, and twisted and plaited handles on the teapot and jugs. And while it is not a sure test, in that all other pottery is not heavy, the Leeds ware was smooth and thin with an unmistakable rich cream glaze and of an extremely light weight.

The period when Leeds pottery was manufactured covered a long period — from 1760 to 1825 — and had two separate markings, "Leeds Pottery" and "Hartley Green & Co." In spite of this it is not always easy to identify accurately, as reproductions have been made over the years which, with the wear and tear of time, are difficult to distinguish from the originals.

Leeds pottery is interesting in that much of it was made during the latter part of the eighteenth century when taste was at its best. After 1825 the pierced designs went out of fashion. Another of its typical characteristics was the "grass edge" on the plates, so called because of the thin green lines painted to resemble grass.

In the ornamental groups were small clusters of figures and animals which were produced by most of the potters. A pair of rams with a lamb in front standing on a base of green grass, a dancing bear which was a common sight in the streets until the nineteenth century, or a lion couchant — all these were popular. Other equally unpretentious clusters

were crinolined ladies grouped about a small table, a boy and girl gaily dressed playing a card game, two small boys accompanied by a dog, and a christening scene with parents, infants, and a clergyman.

In addition to these a host of domestic articles was modelled. Jugs were numerous, usually made in a cream ware with transfer painting, a new process said to have been discovered by a potter, John Sadler of Liverpool. Plates and tiles were painted in this fashion with rural scenes, ships at sea, classical designs and even illustrations from *Aesop's Fables*. Teapots of a distinctive character were made at Castleford in the last decade of the eighteenth century. They had a sliding lid in place of the usual variety and there were groups of figures in relief on the panelled sides.

Some of the jugs showed elaborate border decoration top and bottom, the acanthus and vine leaf being the favorite patterns, or there was sometimes a rural scene painted on the part where the jug bellied out. Jugs made by Felix Pratt who was working circa 1780 to circa 1820 were specially fine. They were made in all sizes, from the very small jug about four or five inches high to others about eight inches in height. They are all well proportioned and of practical charm with lips that pour well and handles that are strong and easy to hold.

Some of the colorful Pratt jugs are decorated with sporting subjects such as huntsmen mounted on horseback, hare and hounds and other animals; and he made a frog mug with a gay picture of the frog in yellow spots.

Later in his career Pratt made many pomade or pot lids printed in colored transfer. In one set of these the "Cries of London" were reproduced. Pratt jugs are still available and with their sturdy vigorous treatment they are worth looking for. Occasionally the base or the neck of the jug was decorated with a gold band and simple flutings, and ears of corn, oak leaves and formalized leaf shapes were also used.

His jugs are the best known of Pratt's output but he also made plates, mugs, teapots, figures and flasks. The prevailing colors were a yellowish orange, and green and blue used with brown and purple. The collector should note that the Pratt figures are more rare than the jugs.

As was the case with fine china which was being made in bulk in England, about the middle of the eighteenth century, potters did not consider it necessary to mark their work. As has been said the most famous of all the potters, Josiah Wedgwood, was one of the first to mark his pieces with the name that was to become so kenspeckle. As it has been in continuous use on dishes dating from the mid-seventeen hundreds until the present day it does not provide a sure guide to those who are trying to distinguish the very old from that which is less old.

It is said that Wedgwood revolutionized the pottery industry. He was descended from a family of potters, and though in his earlier years he made numerous figures brilliantly executed in finely colored enamels, many of these were not marked. He was responsible for removing pottery from what had been considered a kind of peasant art and creating for it a background of elegant sophistication

His figures and statues accounted for only a small part of his output and he is best remembered for his blue and white pieces, with a background of deep blue unglaze ornamented with a raised design in white. His popular cream ware was also decorated in relief, and included pieces for the dinner table, such as cheese dishes, plates, vegetable dishes; he also produced other articles such as trinket boxes, tobacco jars, and vases.

This ware was in such demand that it has never lost its popularity and because of this the original designs have persisted and have not been changed down the years. This makes it difficult to date the different pieces. Much of the modern Wedgwood is very like that of the eighteenth century and consequently the very popularity of the ware has been detrimental to its value which is lower than some other contemporary pottery. Wedgwood also made some black Egyptian pottery as well as his famous Jasper pieces.

Because workmen in those days moved from one factory to another exchanging the secrets of the trade, styles were often merged, making it difficult to identify the work of one special pottery. It is surprising to reflect that while few of the better-known potters' names have been handed down with any degree of prominence, always excepting that of Wedgwood, the names of Staffordshire potters are not all hidden in obscurity.

Josiah Spode was one of these. He was apprenticed to the excellent potter, Thomas Whieldon, the distinguishing feature of whose work was the mingling of colored oxides in his glazes, against a creamy ware thus producing a mottled effect. In 1740 Whieldon set up his own business in a very humble way, in a little row of thatched cottages, but he prospered and for a time was in partnership with Josiah Wedgwood, a somewhat older contemporary who had been born in 1730 and who died in 1795.

No doubt Whieldon learned a good deal from his distinguished associate and he made a fortune and ended up as a Sheriff. Unfortunately he does not seem to have marked any of his pottery, but it is sufficiently distinctive to be readily identified. He specialized in jugs, articles which were always required by all classes, and in teapots, teapoys (tea caddies), and plates of unusual design and pattern.

Having learned his craft under the auspices of Whieldon, Spode was naturally influenced by the latter's type of pottery, but later he acquired works of his own style. He is one of the contestants who claims to have produced the Old Willow pattern which was immediately successful and which has never gone out of fashion.

Spode made many domestic pieces in addition to ornamental pottery and he followed the mode, which by then was increasing, of marking his work. Early Spode is marked simply by the word "Spode" in script or in Roman characters. Later pieces have "Spode" inscribed above a laurel wreath with "Felspar porcelain" written in script inside it. Another mark has "Spode inscribed inside a square and "Stone China" written beneath.

Although he did not make any porcelain during the life-time of Spode Senior, it should be noted that in 1800, shortly after his father's death in 1797, his son began making porcelain as well as pottery. Although both Spode and Wedgwood laid claims to the making of the original willow pattern in England, this was disputed by a fellow craftsman of the time, who was famous for his china as well as his pottery. This was Thomas Minton, who engraved various patterns for Spode including, it is said, the willow designs.

Small group of Toby jugs. (Courtesy John Bell)

Minton also invented the Chinese dragon pattern which he evolved by piecing together some old illustrations of the legend of the unfortunate lovers. This he fashioned together in such a way that it became a story in pictures and thus it was reproduced on the pottery.

After John Dwight whose working life extended from 1671 to 1703, there came to Staffordshire, in the early eighteenth century, two Dutchmen, the brothers Elers, David and John Phillip, who were reputed to be unusually skilled in their craft. They were secretive about what they had learned and refused to pass on their knowledge. But a young apprentice pretended to be deaf and in this way he acquired their secrets. Astbury was born in 1678 and died in 1743 and his pieces naturally reflect the influence of the Elers' work.

After Astbury came Thomas Whieldon, and contemporary with him there was a firm of potters, Ralph Wood and his son of the same name, who worked at Burslem. In the same district were Enoch and Aaron Wood who were perhaps related. Ralph the elder was born in 1716 and died in 1772 and to a certain extent there was a similarity in the work of those potters though each had their own individual touches.

John Walton also worked in Burslem but nearly a hundred years later, and he made many small figures and groups of figures, but he also specialized in Biblical subjects such as Elijah and the Ravens.

Less well known than Walton was Ralph Salt who was making pottery at Hanlem between 1812 and 1834, but the work of the two men bore a distinct resemblance, the one to the other. No account of English pottery is complete without mention of Toby jugs, the first maker of which is said to have belonged to that band of potters which included Thomas Whieldon and the Woods.

The design of the first Toby jug with the portly Toby of genial beaming countenance holding his pot of ale is said to have been a reproduction of Henry Elwes who for his drinking propensities earned the soubriquet "Toby." Another school of though, however, states that the first Toby was Toby Philpot the hero of a popular drinking song.

The characteristic Toby was always jolly and corpulent and the jug was a homely rumbustious piece in strong gay colors with no pretence at refinement representing most vividly the convivial habits of the hard drinking eighteenth century. In a comparatively short time the Toby jug was being turned out by nearly all the potters and it was one of the most successful individual pieces of the time.

While the Tobys differed in detail the general effect of them all was similar. The figure of Toby remained the same — a seated figure in a long coat with deep pockets and buckled shoes, and of course the inevitable pot of ale, and occasionally a barrel and a long-stemmed pipe. This slightly coarse figure was understood by the country folk. The colors were crude but they were strong and clean and the effect friendly and pleasing.

Some authorities give credit to Spode for the introduction of a jug and the accompanying Toby as an increasing rotund gentleman. Toby jugs have remained continuously in manufacture and while it is easy enough to recognize the new productions it is not always possible to identify the old. In searching for an old Toby the thing to look for — but which alas is hard to find — is a jug signed by the potter who made it. Such examples are rare but they can still be picked up.

Towards the end of the century, as an extension of the Toby idea, other jugs representing celebrities of the day were produced. The early specimens were large, usually of two pint capacity, and they included such figures as Admiral Lord Howe, Napoleon, and "The Squire," a gentleman of dignity dressed in a coat of dark blue or green with brown hat and breeches and holding the customary jug of ale.

There were also jugs of anonymous figures. One was "The Drunken Parson" with striped waistcoat, white wig and his hat awry, and another was the red-faced Publican seated on a barrel grasping lovingly a jug of foaming ale. None of these however reached the heights of popularity of the original Toby.

Female Toby jugs were also made, but infrequently. Examples from the nineteenth century may still be found but they were slightly ungainly and they lacked the appeal of the real Toby. They are not in great demand by collectors.

As a change from the figures which the Staffordshire potters had produced in such profusion some potteries began turning out little rustic cottages and turreted houses and castles in gaily colored pottery. Those little "toys" were made in the eighteenth century but they appeared in greater numbers in the nineteenth century when this form of pottery had a distinct vogue.

It is difficult to apportion these little extravagancies into any one category. They are gay and colorful and have a certain charm, but while they are decorative in, for example, a country setting they lack the appeal of pieces which are simpler and less pretentious. One of their features is that they are not really fashioned in proportion and they have a top-heavy effect which destroys their attraction for an artistic collector.

At the same time they are by no means passed by, by the serious lover of antiques and they do fit into the background of a country cottage. In the early nineteenth century when ventilation was still poor and standards of cleanliness doubtful, these small buildings had a definite use, when small cones made from powdered charcoal and gum arabic mixed with various perfumed oils were placed inside the castles and cottages.

These were called pastille burners and they were produced in great numbers by the Staffordshire potters. When they were lit the unpleasant odors of the stuffy background were considerably mitigated by the perfumed wisp of smoke which escaped into the room. From about 1820 until the middle of the century those burners were made for the man in the street, as well as for the more affluent citizen.

In early Victorian days after a non-guttering candle had been invented those miniature houses changed their function and became containers for night lights. To facilitate the placing of those candles, roofs were made in one piece so that they could be easily removed. About the same period the Victorians with their urgency for decoration used small cottages on the chimney piece as ornaments. Elsewhere in the room there were sometimes little churches, though there was possibly a surfeit of decoration already.

Another product of the Staffordshire potters between the end of the eighteenth century and the beginning of the Victorian era was lustre ware. Lustre is a homely piece of no intrinsic value, and when it was first made its most natural background was the kitchen or perhaps the parlor.

Lustre is frankly a country ornament and many of the domestic utensils of an everyday nature were made from it, such as teapots, cups and saucers, salt cellars, and above all, jugs in a variety of sizes. A considerable quantity was made at Leeds including some fine examples of copper lustre teapots which were often decorated in bas relief of turquoise an ornamentation found also in mugs and jugs. Such jugs are in high favor today.

Lustre pieces were first produced by brushing gold oxide solution over the glazed white earthenware of the article to be treated, and this resulted in

Right: Lovely Meissen porcelain snuff box. Gold mounted with rococo scrolls, scattered flowers and figures, *c.* 1750. (Courtesy Asprey)

Left: Gold mounted Chelsea needlecase surmounted by a bust of a girl. (Courtesy Asprey)

a wide range of tones from a vivid yellow to a deep bronze reddened by copper and other alloys, to pale lilac and pink. In later years lustre was applied over reddish brown clay and this gave a richer effect than when it was done against the white background.

Transfer painting which was so popular a decoration on pottery was also used successfully on lustre. A silvery finish appeared about the beginning of the nineteenth century when delicate designs of birds and leafy backgrounds showed up well against the shiny metallic surface.

Lustre was produced in Liverpool and Bristol as well as in the pottery towns but the pieces were unmarked, which is possibly an indication of the value put on them by the makers. A notable feature of lustre is its lightness of weight, whereas pottery is heavy.

Of special interest to modern collectors, at a time when the custom of drinking from mugs has been revived to such a great extent, are the old pottery mugs. These have a distinct flavor of their own though being what they are the shapes vary very little. They tend to be somewhat short and squat,

Rockingham Tea Service, in beautiful colors, outlined in gold. *Circa* 1815. (Courtesy John Bell)

though taller, more slender mugs are not unknown and here and there one comes across the odd barrel shape.

Handles are plain though most graceful, and so sensibly designed that they can adequately support the weight of the mug however full of liquid it may be. Some handles are square rising from the neck of the jug while others soar above it in a pleasing curve, and there are others which follow the pewter type of handle popular at the time and have a swan's neck handle. It is also possible to find, though these are rare, some handles on pewter shaped like a swan's neck. These are known as loving cups. Occasionally there is a handle which is knopped though this is not a common finish.

Most noticeable on the old mugs is the decoration. Sometimes this was on the inside, taking the form of a painted animal such as a little yellow lizard in a brown Rockingham mug, or there might be a spotted toad, in some of the Sunderland mugs. A Leeds example may go one better and have both a lizard and a frog. As these small reptiles were placed far down the mug they were not discovered until the drinker had almost quenched his thirst. A Scottish mug painted with a roistering scene was called the Tam O' Shanter in compliment to Robert Burns.

The ornamentation on mugs should be noted in that it differs so much from all previously accepted forms of decoration. Gone are the dainty birds and floral arrangements, the leaves, the friut and the vegetables. Landscapes were not uncommon and a picture of such items as the first railways — circa 1830 — commemorated contemporary events.

Paintings of well-known figures were also popular, such as an equestrian portrait of the Duke of Wellington, a bust of Gladstone, a head of Disraeli, and the cutting of a new railway line by Lord Derby. This was a later mug, dated 1888. The tall cider mug with straight sides and a thin handle was an extremely pleasing type and when it was decorated by hand instead of transfer painting it was also artistic.

During the Victorian era Bible subjects were often used as illustrations such as "The Prodigal Son," "Jonah and the Whale," and over that period there was a liking for sporting subjects; for example two cocks fighting, a dog chasing a fox, a dog annoying a bull, and on one mug there was a gay, colorful painting of the Hunt near Windsor. These are much more interesting and intriguing generally than the plain modern types.

An amusing production of the eighteenth-century potters was the cow creamer which as the name suggests was a milk jug modelled like a cow. A Delft example was made as early as 1720 and from about 1740 a continuous "herd" appeared from the various potteries, including Stoke on Trent, Rock-

Crown Derby tureens with lids, decorated with flowers, and gilded paw feet. (Courtesy John Bell)

Beautiful Rockingham dessert service. Small bouquets of flowers outlined in gold. Pierced borders. (Courtesy John Bell)

ingham, Derby, and Swansea as well as the well-known Scottish factories at Prestonpans and Portobello.

The cow creamer was made in sections with an inscribed collar and a bell round the neck. Occasionally a saddle was fitted which could be opened to allow for the milk to be poured inside, while the open mouth of the cow acted as the spout. In early specimens the opening was square but by the end of the century the hole was circular. A rather cute touch was the tail twisted over the rump to form the handle.

Although silver cow creamers were made in England about the middle of the eighteenth century, the idea having originated from Holland, it is believed, this unusually teatime piece seems to lend itself more to pottery. It was made throughout the nineteenth century and until the dawn of the present era. The famous makers of Pratt jugs who were making pottery in England until circa 1820 added the cow creamer to their list of products, but the most desirable from the collectors' angle are those made in the eighteenth century, and in their clear fresh coloring and sturdy "honest" appearance they make a firm appeal.

Cow creamers are realistic pieces very well modelled and the colors follow nature. Black, dappled tan, a brilliant orange, a white cow with tan or orange markings — they are all there including an all-white animal.

They are usually made to rest on small rectangular green bases suggestive of the grassy backgrounds of the meadows. When searching for cow jugs examine the lower rims of the plinth on which the creamer stands. These should be unglazed. This little piece ceased to be used for its original purpose about the middle of last century when the principles of hygiene were coming to the fore.

It was practically impossible to clean thoroughly the insides of the creamer and examples produced during the latter part of the century were purely decorative. The collector should take care to avoid modern reproductions which by way of a few dents and knocks on the pottery can be made to give the impression of extreme age.

Many collectors are ignorant of the difference between pottery and porcelain. The two are in categories which are entirely separate though there may be a surface likeness between them. Porcelain is much the finer of the two. It is an exquisite substance and is one of the oldest cultures. It originated many hundreds of years ago in China and this quality of age adds to its compelling interest to any one who is even mildly concerned with the subject.

Some very fine Chinese ceramics were made centuries before Christ and have to be seen in order to

Small decorative dish and two handled loving cup painted with outdoor scenes and gilded handles. (Courtesy John Bell)

Newhall Dinner Service in the Chinese manner. (Courtesy Thomas Love)

appreciate the incredible beauty of the coloring, the astonishing modernity of the design, and the pigment so perfect that in this day and age, with all our accumulated knowledge, it cannot be successfully imitated by our potters.

These items of detail add up to a perfection which cannot be equalled in almost any other man-made article. But while it was being produced and enjoyed in the East for all those hundreds of years, the Chinese kept to themselves the secret of their skills, just as the Venetians and Egyptians had refused to share with the Western nations their knowledge of making glass.

As few travellers from the West reached China it was easy for the Chinese to keep to themselves the discovery of manufacturing this wonderful product and it was not until 1498 that a Portuguese mariner, one Vasca da Gama, opened up a trade route to India. Later this was extended to China and a porcelain factory was set up in Macao circa 1516. It was those early Portuguese traders therefore who brought to Europe the first samples of their wares.

Eventually some specimens reached England and one of the members of the Court of Queen Elizabeth the first presented her with a "porringer of white porselyn garnished with gold," a gift she so much appreciated that in 1596 she dispatched some English ships to the Far East to explore the possibilities of what was to her a new invention.

But in spite of this tremendous Royal effort and the difficulties which were circumvented, the Emissaries of Elizabeth failed to achieve success and it was not for another hundred years that porcelain was known in England to any extent.

One of the amazing points about the arrival of porcelain in the West is that it came not in the guise of a trading commodity, as one would have expected, but rather as an expression of high fashion. After Elizabeth died in 1603 the urge to do deeds of great adventure dropped. The country was unsettled and there are no more tales of ships having been ordered East in the name of beauty and culture.

It was not until the last decades of the seventeenth century when William and Mary were on the English throne that porcelain became, as it were, a viable object. Its popularity with the English was due almost entirely to the Queen. When she married William of Orange she had spent the first twelve years of her married life in Holland.

At that time Holland was culturally ahead of England and had become the main European market for Chinese porcelain which was brought from the Far East by ships of the Dutch East India Company.

When William succeeded to the British throne in 1689 and came to England accompanied by Mary she was still young, not yet thirty, but nevertheless her taste in the arts seems to have been formed. Having realized the importance and beauty of porcelain in Holland and having encouraged the possession of it among her husband's subjects, it was natural that she should find the royal palaces of England very bare in comparison, and should desire to introduce her own modern ideas.

It may be remembered that while Hampton Court Palace had been decorated in the latest fashion about fifteen years earlier, the Inventories of the time do not mention the inclusion of any porcelain. This omission would seem to indicate that it became modish when Queen Mary arrived in England. It may be assumed also that this luxurious ornamentation with its beauty and with its feminine slant was likely to have represented the taste of Mary rather than of William.

As the cult of collecting porcelain received the cachet of royal approval its popularity increased with such speed that there was a feverish anxiety in the more exalted circles to possess at least one piece of the new ware. The mode immediately spread from the Court to the nobles and aristocrats who were only too happy to follow their Queen's example and beautify their homes after the manner she had set.

When one thinks of this sudden acceptance it should perhaps be remembered that the age of china making had not yet reached England and therefore appreciation of the new product was enhanced. Considering the leisured age and how slowly any new ideas caught on, it was surprising, beautiful and all as the porcelain was, that it was launched on the English sea of culture so speedily and with such success.

Chinese porcelain appeared at a most auspicious time, heralding as it did the advent of a new kind

Pair of Bristol Delft plates in lovely condition. (Courtesy Thomas Love)

of furnishing which took more account of effect and general appearance than it had ever done before, and when an age of elegance was about to begin. Had it come to England when the first Elizabeth sat on the throne it is possible it would not have changed the background of the country house to such an extent.

By the time Mary died in 1694 she had accumulated a "greate collection of Porcelain," and while she did not live to witness the full range of its success at least she saw its acceptance by the highest in the land. She saw too the general cultural improvement in the royal palaces and must have known that is was all due to her influence and to the efforts she had made.

It must have given the queen a great deal of satisfaction and pleasure to have set this new trend and to find her own good taste so amply vindicated in the added beauty around her. By the early years of the eighteenth century England's trade was steadily increasing and the moneyed classes were now ordering porcelain directly from China, some of it decorated with their family crests and coats of arms.

The making of porcelain was inspired not as one would have expected by pottery, but by bronze which the Chinese forged as long ago as circa 1,000 years B.C. before the time of Tukankhamen.

To any collector who is anxious to acquire examples of porcelain a certain period of study is essential. For the collector who cannot link up individual pieces with the dynasties which saw their birth, the most attractive thing about Chinese porcelain, initially, lies in the exquisite colors and in the lovely simplicity of the designs. The richness of the sang de boeuf, the delicacy of a vase in famille rose, the vigorous blue and white of a Ming jar with typical dragon decoartion, the subdued coloring of a dish in Chun ware with an astonishingly modern design — these are a joy to live with.

Many of the simple pieces in one color are breathtakingly lovely. One thinks of a Celadon bowl, enchantingly beautiful, not more than about four inches high and of the radiant green shade which apparently the west cannot copy; of a piece of white eggshell porcelain of a fairy-like texture too fragile to touch; and of another shallow bowl in that indescribable yellow which China has made her own. Poems in porcelain.

7

Little Tables

In any study of antiques one of the fascinating points to consider is why each specific old piece came into being. The answer is invariably the same. Furniture, china, silver and the rest — everything indeed, except something that was purely decorative — were first produced because the need for them was urgent and apparent, and the craftsmen of the time becoming aware of the furnishing blanks set about planning how they could meet the requirements.

Never in any one comparatively short space of time were so many new additions made to the domestic plenishings; never so many new pieces of furniture invented by the cabinet makers of the day as there were throughout the eighteenth century. This was a natural, almost an inevitable occurrence.

The seventeenth century bore traces of the rough-living eras that had preceded it. Many of these uncouth ways of life persisted. An English king had been beheaded, his son and heir had to flee the country to France, and the country was racked by civil war. And a usurper, if he did not actually take on the trappings of majesty, ruled the country.

Whatever his merits and whatever his inclinations Cromwell had no time to inspire culture among the citizens, and it was not until Charles II returned from exile in 1660 that the people he was to rule over showed signs of "learning the arts of war no more," and became interested in a more refined way of living.

In the last quarter of the seventeenth century Charles' influence made considerable strides, but styles of living and fashions in furniture move slowly and it was not until almost the turn of the century that changes seemed to sweep over the country like an avalanche. It was as if a heavy door had been suddenly thrown open at the dawn of Queen Anne's reign, heralding not merely a new century but a new age with new customs and habits, as well as new fashions and new ways of doing things. All this brought into being an entirely new background which promised a fascinating vista such as had never been imagined before.

This was particularly encouraged by a change in the structure of society, by the arrival of the new middle class which called for a different more exciting way of life which affected not only the nobles and the aristocrats but more surprisingly the peasants also.

Hitherto money had been almost solely in the hands of the upper classes, but now, thanks to the increasing trade with the Far East — China, Japan and India — a race of acute businessmen sprang up and having acquired fortunes they were anxious to spend them. This resulted in the spread of the fast growing middle class. Anxious to make the most of the money they had made and of the knowledge they had gained, they set about building modern homes for themselves and their families, and they also set about introducing luxury to the interiors.

Outside factors helped enormously to create what was virtually a different world. Chief of these was perhaps a matter of luck, in that an era of almost perfect taste had been born with the new century. There was no lack of money to spend and that, allied to the instinctive feeling of choosing the right accoutrements, which was spreading throughout the land, made a marriage which could not be anything but successful.

There was a third element without which the other two could not have achieved the satisfactory result, and that was the excellence of workmanship which prevailed not only in furniture, the making of glass and silver, in architecture and in all the other crafts as well. A shoddily made article scarcely seems to have been known in the eighteenth century.

But at the beginning of the century the most vital of the new products was furniture. As has already been said antiques were made because the need for them was obvious and urgent, and at no time in history has the response to this been more apparent. The new middle class had its own ideas about architecture and instead of planning houses built on the scale of the large mansions which had been in fashion for centuries, they commissioned instead houses which conformed to the more up-to-date styles which were only just emerging.

Those new houses were more modest not only in the number of apartments but in the size of the rooms. This necessitated smaller furniture and indeed a new type of furniture. Fashions in furniture still move slowly and they moved very slowly indeed nearly three hundred years ago, and yet, in an astonishingly brief time the large heavy pieces which had been in vogue for so long were giving way to new, lighter designs. That furniture was built on smaller lines to suit the different type of house.

One of the obvious results of the smaller pieces was that they presented a notable difference in appearance. There was no question of copying an old piece on a smaller scale but of producing others which were startingly different in line and which gave an arresting different kind of look to the rooms in which they were placed.

This was emphasized by the use of a new wood. Until that time the two chief woods in use were oak and, in a somewhat less degree, walnut. Oak suited the bulky seventeenth-century tables, the aumries or cupboards, and the immense four-poster beds, and the heavy chairs; but the eighteenth-century cabinet makers were quick to recognize that the old pieces did not blend with the new conditions and very soon the demand for it fell off.

Walnut on the other hand was much more pliable and as a wood more decorative; and it was admirable for the smaller Queen Anne pieces, such as the bureaux and desks, chairs, bookcases, commodes and mirrors. It was delightful to look at but one of its drawbacks was that it had not the enduring qualities of oak whose years of service were almost endless. But as the accent of that time was more on elegance and grace of line which were characteristic of most walnut pieces it seemed quite suitable.

Another of its drawbacks was, however, that walnut trees were not large enough to make large furniture such as dining tables and for some time these continued to be made of oak. But there was an unexpected solution to this problem when a new wood, mahogany, began to be imported into England.

To the cabinet makers mahogany was the answer to many of their worries. Like oak it was a hard wood and yet it lent itself to a delicate treatment as walnut did, with the advantage that it had qualities which were both practical and appealing. It could be successfully carved and fretted and while the fact could not be guessed in those early days, its color greatly improved with age, as with the passing of time it faded from a not too pleasing shade of red to a mellow heathery tone.

The great cabinet makers of the age quickly recognized the possibilities of mahogany. It was the favorite medium of Chippendale, Adam and Hepplewhite, and it was employed to a considerable degree by Sheraton, though he did not stick to it so rigorously as his contemporaries did, and was more adventurous in the woods he used which included walnut, ebony, birch and the fruit woods with charming effect.

Chippendale mahogany tripod with raised pierced gallery round the top. Center reeded column. (Courtesy M. Harris)

One of the most notable of the smaller pieces of furniture was the little tea table which could be moved around so easily. Until that era such a piece had not been necessary. There was no special need for it as tea had not been used to any extent. Almost all of the furniture had been large or very large. One of the few exceptions was the oak gate-leg table, but while this was made in several sizes there had not been any gate-legs which were conveniently small.

But now, with the growing popularity of tea as a beverage, tea drinking in the reign of Queen Anne was gradually becoming an established custom. Until the last quarter of the seventeenth century the tea leaf was too expensive for the average house holder and it was not until the dawn of the eighteenth century when the price was dropping that it was fashionable to serve it in the drawing rooms of the haute monde.

And so the small tea table appeared and at once was an essential of better class furnishing. One of the earliest varieties, if not indeed the earliest, was the mahogany tripod. This practical piece was made with a swivel top so that when it was not in use it could be folded up and made to stand against the wall.

The early tripod had a plain circular top with a narrow reeded edge and it rested on a turned column which broke away into three curved spreading legs which sometimes ended in hoof feet. From the first this was a well-proportioned table and judging from the numbers produced it must have been an immediate success. Restrained carving became one of its features, both on the center pedestal and on the legs.

Apart from the carving on the pedestal and the legs the tripod was really a utility article, and it scarcely matched up with the fine silver of the elegant tea equipage. It was not until the middle years of the century that Chippendale, then at the height of his powers, having been born in 1718, conceived a table which was more in keeping with the finely wrought silver and the lovely china which was beginning to be made.

This table he called the pie-crust. It was one of the furnishing triumphs not only of that century but for the next hundred years or so as well. Chippendale was an aristocrat in his line of business. He worked very largely for the upper classes who not only appreciated good taste but could afford to pay for it. Thus his designs were elegant and refined and none expressed this more clearly than the pie-crust table.

The pie-crust was also a tripod, with a circular top set on a supporting column and having three splaying legs, and from this simple basic pattern he made a table which was outstandingly attractive. He did this by carving the edge of the top in a scalloped fashion, in the manner of a pastry decoration. Hence its name, pie-crust.

The edge was slightly raised from the surface and this little gallery helped to keep the tea things secure. The center pillar and also the legs were richly carved and the addition of the carving not only enhanced the general appearance, but it presented a more balanced effect than those tripods which had a plain top, and the details of the simple design added up to unusual elegance.

As with the plain tripods the pie-crust usually had a hinged top and when this was opened up and placed against the well, as was its usual position, its appeal was strikingly apparent.

On some of his smaller tables Chippendale reeded the center stem for a little way down, after which

Mahogany tripod with carved center column and splay feet. Pierced gallery encircling top. (Courtesy John Bell)

Eighteenth-century mahogany piecrust tripod. Fine carving on legs. Reeded center column. (Courtesy John Bell)

Mahogany card table with folding top and paw feet.
Eighteenth century. (Courtesy Thomas Love)

the column swelled out in a slightly bulbous manner, and this was sometimes carved with acanthus
leaves. There were also lion masks and boldly
carved legs which terminated in lion's paw feet. A
point to be noted is that the carving of the pie
crust was usually concentrated on the outer edge of
the surface, leaving the flat top almost entirely free
for the placing of the china.

Tripods continued to be made throughout the
eighteenth century, almost invariably of mahogany,
partly because of its durable qualities and also because it was an excellent medium for the carving
which was so popular. In the nineteenth century
the tripod was still widely used but the decline in
taste in its early years is suggestive in the tripod
with the square top, a table which was more
'utility' than decorative. This was emphasized by
the disappearance of carving on many of the tables.

Attractive as the tripod table was, and as convenient also, in that it could be placed against a
wall when not in use, it lacked the advantages of a

folding table which was fitted with side-hinged
flaps. In the seventeenth century the oak gate-leg
table had made a niche for itself, but it was too
large and heavy and often cumbersome to be
brought out when tea was being served and then removed afterwards. In short it was not a suitable
drawing-room piece.

About 1750 a table built on the same lines as a
gate-leg appeared. It was of mahogany and like
the earlier gate-leg it had two hinged folding flaps,
but owing to its delicate construction its appearance was altogether different. The top was rectangular when opened up and its legs, usually
eight in number, were turned and slender, and finished with small paw feet. As a table it was a huge
success. It could be readily moved about the room
and was ideal as a tea table. Today when a specimen can be found it is small enough to be happily
placed in a modern room.

For a time in the early years of his career much
of the furniture produced by Chippendale bore

Elaborately carved Chippendale wine table with pierced
gallery top. *Circa* 1760. (Courtesy Gregory & Co.)

strong traces of his admiration of Oriental designs
and many of his pieces were so reminiscent of
China, in design and decoration, that they were
referred to as "Chinese Chippendale." This influence was particularly noticeable on his chairs
which had such features as delicate latticed backs,
a fretted bracket between the seat rail and the
frame, and there was sometimes the hint of a
pagoda.

Occasionally, too, his tables also expressed his
love of the Far East. There were many little Oriental touches on his tables. For instance the spandrils

on a small rectangular design were very often styled
and fretted in the Chinese fashion.

One of his small folding tables was so Oriental in
conception that it might have been made in China.
When the flaps were expended it showed a design
closely resembling the lines of a pagoda and the
stretchers which diagonally linked the four straight
legs were pierced and shaped in true Chinese
fashion.

In the center of the stretchers was the kind of
high-pointed finial which if suitably enlarged might
have adorned a Chinese temple. The only arresting

difference was in the wood used. In China mahogany would have not been used to make the table as was the case with the English piece.

One of the most delightful tea tables was an invention of the nineteenth century. It was invariably made of mahogany, and from a longish center rectangular piece two hinged flaps fell on each side. The legs were straight and slender and slightly shaped at the foot, but they had no actual feet and rested on the slightly shaped legs.

A single leg could be pulled out from either of the long sides and these supported the flaps and a flat stretcher fixed to the side pieces rather low on the table linked the shaped end pieces. When the table is opened up it is most roomy and it is unexpectedly solid even in its smaller sizes. While the Sutherland table is scarcely an authentic antique it is one of the most delightful tea tables of the last century and when folded its demands on space are most modest.

A charming little eighteenth-century table is the small tripod wine table. It has never fallen from favor since it first delighted the wine drinkers of two hundred years ago and it continues to be reproduced even today at frequent intervals. It is small and dainty with a reeded edge round the top, splaying legs with a little carving.

The wine table is a modest piece. Again it follows the eighteenth-century preference and is made of mahogany. Its proportions are so good that it needs no elaboration or ornamentation, and it is a joy to possess even if there are still traces on the surface of the wine spilled on it so many years ago.

When old tables have been reasonably well cared for, they have the inestimable quality which comes only with constant care over the years; this is a surface polish called "Patina." This lovely polish is a finish which is the result of patient rubbing — of "elbow grease." There is no other way to achieve it.

It should be stated here, perhaps, that a purchaser of any old piece of furniture which may be marked by wine or water or any other kind of stain should never succumb to the suggestion that it ought to be french polished. It is amazing how many people are ignorant of this, but such treatment will destroy that fine patina which once lost can be restored only by years of regular polishing.

Even if the marks do not entirely disappear the effect is still more satisfactory and the finish more natural looking than if french polish had been applied. In addition a keen and knowledgeable collector of antiques loses interest in a table or chair so treated. Better to endure the disfigurement of a few blemishes on the wood than have the cold shiny look induced by french polish.

Georgian mahogany wine table with open gallery top, resting on a finely carved column and carved tripod base. (Courtesy Gregory & Co.)

Attractive Sheraton mahogany wine cellarette on four small feet. The top has a panel of mahogany beautifully cross banded. (Courtesy John Bell)

Sheraton mahogany Pembroke table. Tapered legs and bow-shaped side pieces. (Courtesy John Bell)

Sheraton nest of tables in satinwood with slender legs, shaped fronts. (Courtesy M. Harris)

Robert Adam, who is better known for furniture in which ecliptical curves and circles predominate than for other pieces which have no curves at all, made some small tables so dainty that they might have been the forerunner of Sheraton designs. One of these was a tiny table little more than two feet in height and having an extending top which was still extremely small when the extension was out, measuring about two feet one inch by one foot three.

It was often made of satinwood with inlay in the center and it had a small shallow drawer with slender tapering legs and thimble feet. It was eminently suitable as a small tea-time drawing room piece or as a dainty bedside table in a bedroom.

Sheraton tables are among the most desirable. His work is outstanding for several qualities which make it more easily identifiable than the work of some of his fellow craftsmen. Inlay is possibly the best-known feature as this is present on practically every piece of furniture which he made. Most of the other cabinet makers of the day used inlay to some extent but most of their furniture was made without it. For Sheraton it was so usual a finish that it was a kind of autograph to all that he made.

But the inlay was discreetly used; a decoration in the most refined fashion. Only rarely on some of his later pieces is there a suggestion that less inlay might have added to the elegance of the piece. His

Late eighteenth-century mahogany work table with shaped top, drawer, and straight legs. (Courtesy Thomas Love)

Sheraton mahogany knife urns with square bases and supported on ball feet. (Courtesy John Bell)

small tables were supremely attractive; a new generation of collectors is growing up, eager to acquire some of those examples, all of which are so eminently adaptable.

Sheraton was noted for the extreme daintiness of his furniture and this is easy to recognize in his little tables. It is also obvious in the chairs he designed, some of which looked so delicate that it seemed they could never stand up to the demands which would be made on them. But his skill lay in constructing chairs which, though they appeared so fragile, were so well designed and constructed from the craftsman's angle that they were as strong and endured as long as others which had a sturdier appearance.

Another interesting quality in Sheraton's work, and one which is not always recognized, is his ability to plan for the future and create furniture

Nest of Sheraton mahogany tables with raised beaded edge. Eighteenth century. (Courtesy John Bell)

Dainty occasional table. Rectangular top with cut corners. Urn shaped stem and carved splayed feet. (Courtesy John Bell)

Canterbury with two shallow drawers and no legs, just four small feet with casters. (Courtesy John Bell)

Sheraton canterbury in mahogany. Fitted with a drawer. (Courtesy John Bell)

which would be welcome many years later. In one of his books of designs there is a sketch of two single beds linked together at the head by a bedhead, made of the same wood as the bed frame — very much after today's designs but which at that time must have seemed revolutionary.

The sketch of this startling new idea was published in 1802 in Sheraton's *Cabinet-maker and Upholsterer's Drawing book,* and it was perhaps looked on as an impractical theory by the clients for whom it was intended. It was certainly not only the ancestor of twin beds but of twin beds which were joined together at the bedhead. Sheraton's name for it was "a summer bed in two compartments." It was a type of four poster with slender posts and a surrounding pelmet and curtains which could be drawn around for privacy.

In addition to the bedhead which extended across the width of both beds, the beds were further linked together at the foot by a delicate rounded arch made of wood to match the beds. The arch was high enough for the occupants to pass under. Advanced as it was the idea seems to have been too far ahead to be accepted at the very beginning of the nineteenth century.

If, however, the "summer bed in two compartments" was not viewed as a practical proposition another of Sheraton's forward-looking ideas did find favor in his own day. This was what we nowadays call a nest of tables and they were produced in sets of graded tables which fitted in to each other. As they were made in sets of four Sheraton called them quartetto tables.

Quartetto tables were usually made of walnut but satinwood was also employed with decorative touches of inlay. Their modern counterparts are copies of those first nests, and the only real difference between them is that the old examples are rather taller than those which are made today. The design is roughly similar with the oblong top resting on turned supports on each side and the sides upheld by yoke feet. Modern nests tend to be square in shape but in the old tables the stretchers are shaped or curved. The genuine Sheraton tables also stand a little higher from the floor than those made today.

Most of these small tables already mentioned were, if not actually planned as tea tables, fitted for

Beautiful Sheraton octagonal breakfast table of walnut.
Cross banding on top. (Courtesy Gregory & Co.)

Sheraton mahogany commode converted into a small
fireside table or a bookcase. (Courtesy Gilbert Morris
& Son)

that purpose. But a host of other small tables with
other uses have come down to us. So many new customs, apart from that of tea drinking, deemed suddenly to demand that a small table should be available.

Besides being an age of elegance and progression
the eighteenth century was above all a feminine
era when for the first time in history the likes and
dislikes of the female of the species were not only
considered but were catered to. Among the few
new pursuits there was notably the vogue for correspondence and many women indulged themselves
by cultivating the art of letter writing. This was
accelerated by the increased improvement in trans-
portation. Roads were improved, the routes taken

by the Royal Mail were extended, and the speed of
stage coaches as well as their reliability began to
rank as items of importance.

All these improvements acted as a spur to letter
writing. Education had made great strides since
the early seventeen hundreds — the ability to read
and write was no longer confined to the few, and
there was a new leisured class of women who were
eager to practice the exciting art of correspondence.
Even in the most remote areas regular stage coach
services bringing up-to-date news of the outside
world were inaugurated. No wonder women took
the chance to express themselves by way of volumi-
nous correspondence.

In turn this fashion affected the furniture. All at

Regency card tables with double folding top resting on shaped column and splayed legs. Rosewood. (Courtesy Thomas Love)

once the writing table became a sine qua non and cabinet makers set about catering for this need. The first writing table created specifically for feminine use was the small Queen Anne walnut bureau with a folding, sloping lid which when open revealed a flat writing surface set against a background of tiers of tiny drawers and pigeon holes, just like the fitments of a bureau as we know it. The little drawers had ivory knobs for handles and the piece was finished with two long drawers resting on modified cabriole legs. The whole piece was very small and dainty.

This type was succeeded by a much more practical design which was so admirable that it has never been altered, save in minor details. It also was small, perhaps less than three feet long. The chief

change was in the lower part of the piece which had graded drawers reaching to the floor and it was finished with bracket feet instead of legs. Both varieties of bureaux are extremely rare and are costly to acquire and because of this they are out of reach of most collectors.

In choosing a piece like this the insides of the drawers should be examined. On a genuine Queen Anne desk with original handles these are attached to the wood by sharpened wires which pierce the drawer and are then folded back flat in opposite directions, a simple and adequate device to keep the drawer handle securely in position.

As handles take so much of the wear and tear of a piece they frequently have to be replaced by others of a modern type. When this is so it should

Mahogany square topped table on turned column and
splayed legs. (Courtesy Thomas Love)

not be presumed that the piece itself is not an antique. At the same time it is astonishing how often
the original handles with their fittings are found
on a Queen Anne bureau or chest of drawers.

There was endless variety in the arrangement of
the interiors of those litle bureaux. The tiny
drawers and compartments were meticulously finished and in some of the finer examples were
finished with a serpentine front.

Later in the century Sheraton expended his ingenious skill in designing small bureaux — and
large ones too — with secret hiding places, some of
them so well concealed that their contents lay un-
discovered for many years. A feature of those early
small bureaux is that they were obviously made

with feminine requirements and they are most desirable today, not least because they can be placed
so easily in a small apartment.

In the early years of Queen Anne's reign a superb
small writing table was produced. It was different
from the bureau type in that it had a flat table top
beneath which was a shallow longish drawer, and
beneath that again on either side a tier of deeper
drawers reaching almost to the floor and a kneehole space between and standing on bracket feet.
There was an arched recess containing a cupboard
for important documents and the piece was much
enhanced by finely shaped brasses and keyholes.
Bail handles were usual but sometimes the drop
handle was used instead.

Early nineteenth century rosewood table. Hinged flaps
at each side of center. Double supports and stretchers
on shaped feet. Drawers in center. (Courtesy Thomas
Love)

Rosewood Regency table with folding flap at each end.
Inlay on drawers and on center platform. (Courtesy
Thomas Love)

Kidney-shaped dressing table with turned legs. Mahogany. *c.* 1800. (Courtesy Thomas Love)

When mahogany succeeded walnut in the time of the Georges the style of bureaux and writing tables hardly changed. It was about this time or rather earlier that the need for a special table at which a woman could make her toilette was recognized, and some of the flat-topped writing tables were slightly altered for this purpose. So nearly alike were they that at a casual glance the one might be taken for the other. There was still the arched recess with the recessed cupboard but as it was now intended for hats it was more spacious than the one in the writing table.

The flat top of the dressing table was not always wide enough to accommodate the new swing toilet mirrors newly in fashion, and when this was so a wall mirror was hung behind. It was really a delectable little piece and must have been a most advanced idea to the women of the early seventeen hundreds for whom a dressing table had hitherto consisted merely of a casual table with no additional accessories.

So few examples of this delightful piece are available today and when they are, the cost is so prohibitive that most collectors can have only an academic interest in their attractions.

Right down through the ages women have exercised their skills in embroidery both ecclesiastic and domestic but not until the eighteenth century was the need for a receptacle for the sewing materials recognized and the small work table made its debut. Much fine embroidery had been produced in earlier centuries by the women of noble lineage, but much of it was large — counterpanes, curtains, and the like — and it was probably kept in deep aumries or cupboards when it was not actually being stitched.

By the eighteenth century the leisured middle class was increasing and to fill in unoccupied hours by working delicate stitchery of a more personal nature became a fashionable pursuit. Tapestry and covers for chairs were comparatively small pieces and it was essential to have a small compact container in which they could be kept conveniently at hand. The cabinet makers responded by producing an outcrop of small tables planned to hold the current pieces of needlework along with the requisite wools and threads.

Designs of those tables varied. The most convenient was a skeleton folding table made from mahogany, birch or one of the fruit woods, with a deep bag of silk or velvet for the sewing suspended between the folding wood ends. This was light in weight and could be carried about the house as required and this design has remained popular. The snag about it was that it was not so much a table as a workbag.

Sheraton entered the field and turned out some delightful types. One in satinwood had an eight-sided top with a hinged lid which formed the actual box. It was bound by a narrow band of inlay, the inlay repeated on the slender legs which splayed slightly towards the base. Stretchers were fitted diagonaly between the legs with a dainty finial in the center and the box finished with a small lock of ivory.

Another Sheraton work table consisted of a much deeper compartment which was capable of taking a considerable quantity of sewing. It was made of walnut bordered with rosewood and had a charming decoration of inlaid panels in front and at the sides.

In this table the legs were turned and again they splayed at the base. This ornamental and most useful table must have been much in demand as it is now rare. A similar design of the same period was carried out in satinwood, edged with ebony, which was a favorite finish with Sheraton.

Also rare is the late eighteenth-century work table in papier mache. The usual design had a flat box top with a deep recessed compartment falling from this in the manner of a workbag. The table stood on two turned legs and the curved ends were linked by a turned strecher. When it can be found, this makes a delightful work table, the bright colors of the papier mache showing up against the black shiny background of the "mashed paper" producing an effect which is at once gay and arresting.

Among the small tables that can be easily housed in the limited space of modern rooms a less usual type is the rectangular table. This is not an ultra small table and it is ideal for a narrow hall or passage way or it may act as a dressing table in a not-very-big guest room. It may even serve as an occasional dining table for one person.

Chippendale was one of the first of the craftsmen to sponsor this table. He made it in walnut as well as in mahogany. It is fitted with a long drawer or sometimes two shallow drawers fitted horizontally, and usually the top is made to extend a little over the frame. The legs are slender and tapering and there is often reeding on the legs and on the edge of the top.

During his Chinese period Chippendale introduced Oriental touches on such tables especially on the spandrils, and on the fairly thick legs he had a decoration of perpendicular reeding. There were sometimes fret brackets linking the under frame with the legs. In similar tables made by Sheraton he varied his design by having delicately turned legs and fluted carving — also the inevitable inlay.

Hepplewhite also produced some small rectangular tables that were reminiscent of Chippendale's designs. Others were copied later in the century by Sheraton. The legs on Hepplewhite tables were often typical of Chippendale while the turned legs which he used after a period of absence were very like those on Sheraton examples.

Much of the appeal of the small eighteenth-century tables lies in the fact that they were pioneers of their kind. But they possess the inestimable quality of a dateless appearance, and after two hundred years of constant use they still remain entirely up-to-date and modern and extremely suitable for the requirements of this present generation.

It is interesting to realize that as the years of the century went on, many little tables appeared which had no special characteristics to denote their maker. The notable cabinet makers of the time issued books of their own designs and these gradually circulated about the country and were copied by country craftsmen, who though quite unknown were nevertheless excellent workmen and good copyists.

Consequently while many of these small tables are in a sense hybrids they should be admired for what they are, delightful pieces of good design and not despised because they cannot be labelled with the tag of a great cabinet maker.

Though not quite in the category of the very small table an admirable type is the eighteenth-century circular tripod drum table. It is usually made of finely marked wood and may also have an inlay design in the center. The small drawers surrounding it are shallow. The center column is turned but the splayed legs attached to it are square and are finished with casters.

8

Pewter

Few articles by their very existence are as reminiscent of bygone days as pewter. In the Middle Ages it was held in high esteem domestically as china had not yet been invented and the amount of earthenware available was limited for use in kitchen and dining room.

Pewter was used on everyday occasions for all kinds of dishes — cups, plates, porringers, platters and cruets, alike in castle and cottage. For best use the aristocracy had vessels of silver while the poorer classes who could not afford pewter, much less silver, ate and drank from articles of treene (wood) or from horn.

Even by the end of the fifteenth century when pewter was being produced in greater quantity it was still too expensive for the poor. Gradually, however, as more of the metal appeared on the market it became cheaper, and as a result was within the reach of most grades of society and from then on, it was in widespread use until about the end of the eighteenth century.

After that its popularity waned. Its fall from favor was due to two factors: one was the importation of pottery from abroad; the other was the setting up of factories in England for the home manufacture of china and also of pottery. Both these substances must have been a delight to the palate and to the eye, hitherto somewhat starved of color; and to housewives the fact that they were easily cleaned raised them to a desirability beyond pewter.

With the advantage of hindsight it is sad to reflect on the amount of pewter which for various reasons was thrown out towards the end of the eighteenth and the beginning of the nineteenth centuries, much of it made in the seventeenth and eighteenth centuries by the most skilled pewterers. It is fortunate for the present generation that our ancestors retained at least a proportion of the pewter in their kitchens and sculleries.

After pewter was banished from the domestic scene and replaced by pottery and china it was still used, as formerly, in the inns and taverns of the land and for modern collectors this is a cause for gratitude. Those small graded measures and mugs, those tankards and jugs some with handles and some without, some possessing hinged lids, and others lidless, are more intriguing possessions today than any cup or dish or cruet.

It is those tavern pieces, gently polished to a soft gleam and set on the shelves of an old oak dresser, which achieve a mellow charm in a hall or dining room. It may be said here that in a sense pewter is a kind of holiday antique. Much of it is small and can be easily transported home. One or two graded measures or an odd beer mug make a delightful gift, while a jug or mug of any size makes an excellent flower container.

A piece likely to appeal to the collector is the pewter plate, and it should be noted that plates and dishes are not synonymous. The dish is much larger and is usually circular, though it is sometimes oblong. Its use was to take the meat course from the kitchen to the dining room. Such dishes were sometimes called "pye plates" or "dishes for rabbittes."

The plate on the other hand had the same meaning as it has today, being the article from which the food was eaten. The plate is one of the most attractive pewter productions with its slightly curved broad rim. A collector who is beginning to acquire pewter should realize that a plate is most desirable when it is quite plain, without scroll or decoration.

Ornamented pewter is usually of European extraction and is almost certainly of less value than English pewter. Some English plates, however, are reeded and this unobtrusive touch does improve the general appearance. Another not displeasing addition is the initial of the owner placed either on the edge of the plate or underneath it. There may be two sets of initials indicating that the owners are married.

Candlesticks of pewter are rich in aesthetic appeal, but because the metal is soft and has suffered from the close proximity to heat, they are not plentiful. The single stick is fairly easily picked up but a pair has to be searched for.

Candlesticks made about the end of the eighteenth century and for some decades afterwards are fitted with circular or octagonal grease trays to match the different bases. The trays are usually fitted near the top. Examples made in the early years of the reign of Charles I resemble an inverted drinking cup with the addition of a tubular socket. Others have what is termed a "salt" base which means that the base of the candlestick which is allied to the stem not only *seems* to be an upturned salt cellar but has actually been made for this purpose.

Some candlesticks have a chalice base and this also is a piece of pewter designed for two purposes, as the base could be used as a drinking cup when necessary. Perhaps because of their hard-wearing qualities domestic candles were more frequently of brass than of pewter.

In design the pewter crandlestick tends to follow those sticks made in brass rather than in silver. They were in use in churches from an early period, possibly about the fourteenth century, and were produced in all sizes. Brass ecclesiastical candlesticks were very tall whereas those of pewter were of more modest proportions.

In later church specimens there was a movable nozzle to facilitate the easy removal of burnt out candle ends, and occasionally there was a wire arrangement fitted inside the center of the base, which continued upwards inside the stem till it reached the socket. When it was pushed from the base it forced out the last remnant of the candle. This was a common fitment in brass candlesticks both domestic and church types and its existence being a proof of age adds to the value of the stick.

The bell-shaped candlestick is an intriguing little piece. Its name describes its appearance and it stands from ten to twelve inches high. About halfway down the stem there is a tray fixed so that it can catch the grease from the candle and the candlestick may be placed safely on a polished surface of oak or mahogany or walnut without causing any harm. There is a simple variety of candlestick with a circular reeded base with a couple of knops near the top and this is comparatively easy to find. Another frequent feature is the baluster stem.

Not unlike the bell-shaped design is the trumpet candlestick save that it swells out in a wide sweep in the fashion of a trumpet. An attractive design usually found in brass is fairly tall with knopped stem; it rests on a base which may be circular, square or octagonal.

It is interesting to reflect that pewter was widely used in colleges and churches, and a point worth noting is that its importance was such that it was entered in the Inventories of the time, not only throughout the Middle Ages but in the seventeenth and eighteenth centuries as well. After about the middle of the eighteenth century, by which time china and pottery were establishing their own niche in domestic ware, the manufacture of pewter began to dwindle. It was still found in the kitchens of country houses and in cottages and farmhouses, however, and its use was continued in the taverns and inns about the country for a considerable time.

The coming of the nineteenth century saw the influx of fresh customs, and the domestic articles of pewter, which had originated several hundred years earlier and which were still in vogue, were now reckoned as old fashioned. The demand for pewter was waning.

The making of pewter was a guarded skill in England and there was a Pewterers' Company as long ago as 1348. About a hundred and thirty years later a charter was given to the Company by Edward IV and this confirmed the right of assay and the premises of craftsmen could be searched.

According to Mr. Cottrell every action of the early pewterer was governed by and regulated by his guild. He was not to work at nights, first because of the noise which the workmen made on the metal, and secondly because good work could not be performed in the dim artificial light of those early days. Every particle of pewter had to be tested by standards kept at the Pewterers' Hall for that purpose before he could put up his goods for sale, and no man was allowed to employ workmen other than apprentices who were freemen of the guild.

English pewter was of a notably high standard and an early restriction in favor of keeping up the quality made sure that no pewter should be brought into London to be sold, without being assayed. There was a strong feeling of fellowship among the workers and it was this anxiety on their part to produce only good work which not only ensured their own skills but which helped them to stand together as a band of pewterers against less official workmen. Of these there were many — hawkers and tinkers and casual laborers — who saw in the pewtering business a comparatively easy way of making money without the supervision which the guild members had to endure.

H. J. L. J. Masse states that in the reign of Richard II — 1377–1399 — the pewterers complained bitterly that their business was being injured by pedlars and tinkers going around the country recasting the worn out or damaged articles brought to them by their customers. The official pewterers said that the pedlars ruined the alloy with lead so that it was not worth a quarter of the price which it fetched.

It appears that this adulteration with lead was a secret source of profit to these casual workmen as they charged very little for the recasting of the pewter. It is not known accurately but it is presumed that vagrant wandering workers dealt chiefly in domestic articles, recasting such pieces as plates, dishes, and small "bolles" or bowls, as well as saucers and platters.

In order to detect those tinkers who cheated by selling light weight King Edward IV gave the Pewterers Company its first charter by confirming the right of assay and giving the power to search the premises of the salesmen. Immediately this charter was made known, many of the unofficial pewterers joined the London company. The right of searching premises in distant parts of the country was both difficult and costly but it helped to maintain the high standard of workmanship.

The marking of pewter is a thorny point as many of the old pieces bear no marks at all. And yet in 1503 it was made compulsory by an Act of Parliament to mark all pewter. At the same time the sale of pewter and brass anywhere except in an open market or in the premises of a pewterer was forbidden. Such rules helped to maintain the standard of manufacture and helped the maker to recognize pewter and identify its origin.

The mark on pewter by the pewterer is referred to as the "touch" and varies according to the size and type of piece. Sometimes the full name of the maker was given; at other times merely his initials. Very often because of the softness of the metal these have become indistinct with constant usage, and because of this, one piece of pewter may bear the touch of more than one owner.

In addition to the actual name on the base there may also be other devices such as a sun in splendor, a crowned rose, a dolphin, a crescent or a moon, two hearts, or an angel on a globe. The mark "X" is indicative of a superior quality of pewter but the lack of it does not mean that the pewter is poor. A crowned rose sometimes accompanies the "X."

Pewter is made from tin with the addition of brass, lead, copper, and antimony or bismuth used in varying degrees. The basic component of all grades of pewter is tin, and the greater proportion of tin and the less proportion of lead, the better is the appearance of the finished product. This explains why some mugs and measures have a silvery effect while others remain heavy and dull looking no matter how much they may be polished.

Good pewter can be polished till it shines like silver but this is not considered advisable, for while pewter should be bright it should not suggest an imitation of silver. In spite of some opinions to the contrary it should be cleaned regularly. To leave it dull and dark robs it of much of its charm.

To revert to the touch marks. The mark of the crowned rose could only be used by permission of the London Goldsmiths' Company. It should be noted however that the rose and crown is not a touch confined to English pewter but is found also on Scottish examples as well as on some European pieces from Holland, France or Germany.

Initials were sometimes engraved or stamped on such pieces as domestic plates, indicating not only the names of former owners, but if the initials were duplicated, of a married couple. Initials were often found on flagons of the larger types, but rarely on smaller examples. When a crown was used, as on a Tappit Hen, this was probably a government stamp which had been placed there as a guide to the accuracy of the measure.

As might be expected there were specialists among the pewterers. Some workmen were employed only on heavy articles, including table dishes, while "triflers" worked at lighter wares — spoons, forks, buckles, buttons and toys — and "hollow ware" men were occupied with pots, tankards, and the smaller measures. At first the "hammer men" and coppersmiths were included among the pewterers but later they formed an organization of their own.

In spite of all the precautions that were taken to keep the business of pewtering straight and honest, including the use of false scales being forbidden, complaints were still being made in the reign of Henry VIII "that many simple and evil disposed persons" had become in modern parlance receivers for pewter that had been stolen. Expressed in the terms of the day "knowing thieves and other pickers that steal pewter and brass . . . bring it to privy places or into corners of cities or towns and sell it for little or naught."

Those "evil doers" also mixed good metal with bad and sold it as good stuff. In an endeavor to remedy these faults an act was passed restricting the sale of pewter to "open fairs and markets or in the craftsmen's own dwelling houses." There was also an effort made to confine the making of pewter to Englishmen. "No strangers born out of this realm were to be retained as apprentices or journeymen."

By the early years of the seventeenth century pewter was commonly used for domestic articles, many of which were new to the trade. Among these were "deep vessels," "basons" "Bowles," "pastie plates," 'plain' pottes and other pottes, also spoons and ladles, egg cups and strainers, as well as other pieces whose names are unknown to this generation.

The progress of pewter had been stormy but the pewterers were shrewd and their rules were wisely made. Not only did they fix the price of the pieces which were for sale, but they also arranged what price should be paid when old pewter was exchanged for new. Pewterers were also modest and the praising of their wares was deprecated. When one pewterer, Jonas Durand, wanted to add to his "touch" "nephew of Taudin," this was forbidden. It was also forbidden for pewterers to add their addresses though, later, this practice was allowed.

The excellence of English pewter was known and appreciated in Europe and this was partly due to the fine quality of Cornish tin which was used in its manufacture. In the late seventeenth century the metal was so widely in use that women workers were taken on. This was so especially in the country districts, far from London. There were several women pewterers at that time in York.

Women also worked at the trade in France as early as the latter part of the fourteenth century. Unfortunately the standards of the fineness of pewter cannot be traced today with any accuracy but these were certainly strict. One of the rules of the York Company stated that "none of the said crafte shall hereafter cast anye vessel but of good and fine metell and shall not put any sowder (solder) therein among the same."

No collector of pewter can ignore the existence of Britannia metal which in appearance so much resembles pewter that to a beginner it might well be mistaken for it. But once one has learned to identify the one from the other it is almost impossible to confuse them. Pewter has a delightful mellow sheen while Britannia metal faces the world with a hard cold look in an unprepossessing greyness.

Britannia metal is an alloy which is a kind of debased form of pewter, rather like an undesirable relation. It is not nearly as old as pewter; and it made its first appearance in England about the middle of the eighteenth century. Like pewter it is composed of tin with the addition of antimony and a little copper but the result is a dead-looking metal which no amount of rubbing and polishing can transform.

Apart from the color, the designs used in the two metals are different. It is not easy to pinpoint exactly what this difference is but it is quite definite and after a little practice it is easy enough to learn what is pewter and what is Britannia. The two metals should not be mixed and should never be displayed together on a shelf or cupboard.

In the poorer parishes of the United Kingdom Britannia was sometimes used for communion plate and there exists in the Museum at York an early example stamped with the name of Dixon and Sons, and dated 1751. It was also used for Communion tokens in the early Scottish Presbyterian kirk. Those were copies of the lead tokens produced as early as 1550 — at the suggestion of Calvin, it is said — by the French Calvinists.

In the more remote districts of Scotland they were handed round the congregation for use at the Sacrament as the Communion season drew near. Later tokens were of pewter but Britannia was most frequent. In shape they were usually square, about an inch in width, or oblong, but they were sometimes circular or hexagonal and the very early specimens were marked by the name of the parish church and the minister. Or if space was too limited to allow the full name to be entered there was a "K" for kirk, a "C" for church, and an "M" for magister or minister.

Gradually the initials of the minister were considered of greater importance than those of the church. In small country parishes where tokens were scarce they were shared when necessary with other communions. Though a few tokens may still be found in out-of-the-way country parishes these have given way almost entirely to the ticket or piece of cardboard which acts as admission to the Communion service. It is interesting to note that in pre-token days a pasteboard card was used so that the modern small card is a reversion to the original custom.

The communion token, no matter of which alloy it is made, is the smallest article made either of pewter or Britannia. It is also one of the most romantic, having a close contact with the churches of Geneva, Holland, and the Reformed church of France; in addition it has a strong Scottish connection.

In the seventeenth century, in the Covenanting times, the token was distributed among church members to ensure their admittance to Conventicles when these were held on lonely hillsides within close range of the enemy and in terror of the worshippers' lives. It was vital that there should be an obvious distinction between genuine members and gate crashers who might betray those meetings of the Covenanters to the government.

In any chapter on pewter there should be a mention of such delightful pieces as christening bowls, chalices, alms dishes, patens and flagons, and the important little quaich. Decoratively any of these is a great asset to a furnishing scheme when it is well displayed. The larger pieces were of ecclesiastical origin while the quaich on the contrary is a drinking vessel, shallow and shaped like a deep saucer with ears or "lugs" at the sides.

But even though the quaich is a drinking cup it has certain links with the churches. In tiny churches which possessed a minimum of plate, it was occasionally used for the collection, and on rare occasions it acted as a sacramental cup. It is found in several sizes, as small as about two inches in diameter, or it may be a good deal larger resembling the English porringer.

The kirk flagon is a lovely reminder of the early seventeenth century when it first appeared in England. At that time it was made of silver but as silver became scarce owing to the condition of the times, a good deal of it was replaced by the more modest metal. During the reigns of the two kings, Charles I and II, some beautiful flagons were produced — tall and tapering with a knopped lid. Sometimes the base was slightly stepped.

Pewter was used to a great extent in churches. Baptismal ewers with accompanying basins, flagons, chalices and patens, altar lights, shrine lamps and ciborium — this was a vessel closely resembling a chalice with an arched cover — holy water cups; all these were found in churches throughout the land.

Some of the Scottish flagons are particularly pleasing with their flat, graceful handles, and thumb pieces, similar to those found on tankards and measures of the period, may still be seen in small remote churches where they are used in addition to the ecclesiastical silver plate or instead of it if the church is too poor to afford silver. Flagons were in use before alms dishes. Alms dishes are usually quite plain but occasionally there may be an ecclesiastical emblem engraved on the rim, such as I H S with a cross above it.

Among the more rare church pieces is the chalice. It is also one of the earliest and to begin with was made of gold or silver. It was only when the more precious metals could not be obtained that pewter was used; and this must have been a frequent occurrence for many of the smaller churches were not in a position to afford gold or silver.

Early chalices were fashioned like small communion cups with a baluster stem and a small spreading foot. The later type which is known nowadays consists of a much larger cup, rather like a rummer, and this slopes down to the baluster stem finishing in a domed base.

While chalices are rare so also are patens. The paten is a plate resting on a short thick supporting stem and is used to hold the bread at the Sacrament. The original design was plain but there is reeding on some examples, both on the edge of the plate and on the stem. Some fine pewter patens were lost during the nineteenth century when there was a reckless melting down of old pewter to be remade into other articles, and presumably many church pieces were destroyed in this way. Measures and mugs were also lost to posterity but a greater number still exist possibly because there were more of them than of church pieces.

One of the most desirable of old church pieces is the christening bowl which while it is ecclesiastical has no special resemblance to church plate. It is plain and rarely has any engraving or applied ornamentation on the inside or outside. The shape of the basin is good, not too high and often having a fairly broad flattish rim which is sometimes reeded and thus lends character to the piece.

With one or two exceptions, including plates and some dishes, certain snuff boxes and the quaich, domestic pieces are less attractive to the collector than either church plate or little mugs and measures from the taverns. These small measures indeed have almost become domestic and can be made to look at home in almost any room of the house.

Pewter once collected must be displayed, and this implies the possession of a certain amount of space. It is most satisfactory against a background of oak preferably an old dresser, and it also looks well against pine. It loses a good deal of its appeal if it is displayed against mahogany and it should never be laid out in conjunction with walnut which is far too elegant a wood to blend happily with the more homely metal.

A delightful asset in a room or in the hall is an old dresser with a display of gleaming pewter placed if possible where it can catch the light. If plates are to be shown they should be tilted at an angle so that they may reflect the sunshine. The possession of some really good pewter makes it difficult to resist the temptation to arrange on the dresser as many pieces as can be shown. But overcrowding is never successful and to do so is apt to detract from the aesthetic charm of each individual piece. On the other hand too few pieces suggest a sparseness that is equally undesirable.

Measures of all kinds are admirable pieces to collect. They seem to lend themselves to being arranged in rows or in little groups, and they blend admirably with practically all other types, such as plates, dishes, tankards and mugs; and they are even in accord with the more dignified church pieces. A Tappit Hen will also stand quite happily at the end of the row of this heterogeneous selection.

The baptismal bowl is one of the easiest pieces to place. Its lines are so simple that it suggests no special period and it tones very well beside tavern pieces both large and small.

In any serious collection care should be taken in the choice of measures. The quality of the pewter should be considered so that where several mugs or jugs are arranged together the colors tone, but one has a sense of satisfaction in arranging beside each other little families of graded measures, or jugs and mugs which have some kind of affinity.

If no dresser is available to house the pewter, hanging shelves may act as a substitute particularly if there are several plates which should never be made to lie flat but should stand or rest in an upright position. Shelves should be wide enough to allow the plates comfortable space without fear of an accident. There should also be some kind of support at either end of the shelves and also at the bottom, so that the pewter will not fall off.

It is perhaps not entirely unnecessary to add that if plates or dishes are to be hung on the wall as a decoration there should never be a hole drilled in the edge to take the cord or wire. To do so is nothing short of vandalism, as the boring of the opening destroys the value of the piece. If it cannot be otherwise supported then it should be made to stand on the floor, resting against the wall. This is quite a pleasing method of displaying plates.

Another method of displaying pewter to good advantage is to arrange it in an open shelved cupboard, with the proviso that there is no glass in the cupboard. When this is done there should be no other metal beside the pewter. No copper, silver or brass! Neither should there be any china or pottery on the same set of shelves.

While it is not easy to recognize the different ages of pewter — that is in the absence of any marking — there are some guides which make it possible to detect the approximate date of its manufacture. These are to be found in the shapes of the pots and mugs and in the features of the lids, handles and thumb pieces. These can be most informative.

The pewter pot came into use in England about the middle of the seventeenth century when it probably replaced mugs of treene, leather and horn. At first these pots were not specially decorative but one item of interest was the fact that the names of the tavern and of the landlord were nearly always engraved on the body of the pot. On some specimens there were also engraved on the flat handle the initials of the landlord and his wife.

During the last couple of decades or so of the century pots were a little more ornamental. The name of the maker was still there, and in addition there was the date of its manufacture, and occasionally there was a narrow ribbed band of decoration near the rim of the pot, and a broader rim at the bottom. Sometimes the ribbing was vertical and at other times it was almost crescent shaped which was extremely graceful. It is one of the few types of decorated English pewter which is really pleasing.

Those early pewter pots were sturdy little pieces, extremely strong and tapering slightly towards the top and having a sturdy base. The handles in the early specimens began at the very edge of the rim and then curved down almost to the foot of the mug in a shape rather like an inverted "S." Examples which were made about the end of the century had handles which were slightly shorter and had a less ebullient swing. No lids were found on these pots. They were simply drinking vessels.

Tavern pots were still being made in the eighteenth century and they often had reeding around the bottom and on the body also. About this time there was a further cut in the size of the handles, which though still quite adequate were nearer and more modest than the earlier types.

Thumb pieces are interesting. The thumb piece on a measure is the small upward projection from the lid which acts as a purchase when it is pressed in the act of raising the cover. In different parts of England and Scotland and also in Europe thumb piece designs varied. It should be noted that certain pewterers, particularly those employed in Scotland, were often conservative in their methods and were inclined to follow the shapes originated by their immediate predecessors, rather than launch out on new styles of their own.

Apart from this, designs varied throughout the land. There was a strong school of pewterers working both in Glasgow and in Edinburgh. This resulted in minute differences in the same piece. From examination of those specimens it is possible to recognize where each has been made. In tankards dating from the middle of the seventeenth century until about 1720 it is rare to find two thumb pieces exactly similar. There is always something different — little features which can be very revealing.

Belonging to that period is the love-bird thumb piece which is formed by two birds sitting facing each other. Very rare and therefore difficult to find is the wedge-shaped variety which was made much earlier, in the reign of Henry VIII. A Scottish thumb piece which was produced in Edinburgh as well as in Glasgow is the shell type, a decorative piece.

On the Scottish baluster measure there is fixed the ball thumb piece; and one that decorated tankards for many years was the chair-back thumb piece. After this came the "open variety" which was popular though it possessed no special characteristic

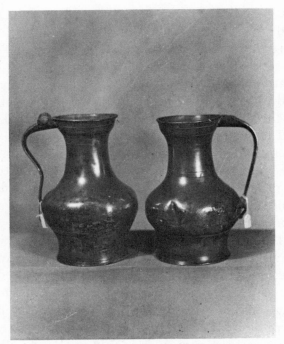

Two Scottish pewter measures. Seventeenth century.
(Courtesy John Bell)

Scottish pewter measure with shell thumb piece. (Courtesy John Bell)

apart from the open loop.

Handles should also be closely studied. On such pieces as tappit hens, measures, flagons and the like they are most important and help to pinpoint the date of their manufacture. Many of the early Stuart tankards of the seventeenth century were finished with a swan's neck handle and this remained in favor for about fifty years, and was still in use with slight variations until about the end of Queen Anne's reign.

The swan's neck is one of the most beautiful of pewter handle designs, particularly when they were first made, when they were elegant and slender. Later examples had a thicker handle and this was less pleasing. On some designs the handle split at the end into a double terminal and this was called the "double handle." It was a popular type and had a long life, from about 1730 till about the middle of the nineteenth century.

Certain handles of the late seventeenth century had a flattened curve and bulbous terminals were typical of the time. In some old Scottish pewter mugs and jugs and flagons, there are handles with a blunt or rudimentary split end, while in English pieces of the same period the handle ends with a sweep like a fish tail.

Lids of measures can also be informative as to the age of the piece. Early Stuart lids or covers can be recognized from the shape which at that time was extremely simple being quite free from moldings and having a lid which rises only a little from the level of the narrow flat brim. About the middle of the seventeenth century there was a change in design. The cover rose higher, and in place of the vertical sides there were convex moldings on the top which was still flattened. During the latter years of the century the dome was raised more definitely and it had a center blob which the earlier lids lacked.

This not very pleasing style was followed by a double domed lid, and like its predecessor it also was mounted on a narrow brim which sometimes had a serrated projection and sometimes not. The double dome existed from the reign of the Stuarts until well into Georgian times. It may be noted that in this lid the dome moldings began to be made flush with the outer edge.

Designs of the small measures should also be

studied, those without covers as well as the lidded measures. These have been dealt with fairly extensively in *Antiques for the Modern Home* by the author of this book, as have the larger measures, including the Tappit Hen and the Normandy Flagon. The latter is a large piece of French extraction as its name indicates, and though there is a surface resemblance between its general appearance and that of the Scottish Tappit Hen they vary considerably. The Tappit Hen is by far the more decorative of the two.

The name Tappit Hen does not apply to one measure alone but is bestowed on several measures which have many points in common. The Tappit Hen is lidded and crested and slightly waisted, and is found in sets of three of varying sizes. The specimen without the crest is ascribed as being earlier than the others. But with or without a crest the Tappit Hen is a delectable possession.

9

Tea Drinking and Its Appurtenances

When tea drinking first appeared in England it was one of the most revolutionary customs of that or any age. Tea had been imported earlier to Europe from the Far East but it was not introduced into England as an acceptable commodity until the latter half of the seventeenth century.

Samuel Pepys who was one of the most enthusiastic "triers out" of new fashions — he purchased a mirror for his wife before most of his contemporaries had even seen that new invention — recorded in his Diary in 1660 that he had "tasted the new beverage, China tea" which at that time was pronounced "tay."

The arrival of the teapot however did not coincide with that of the beverage, and the earliest known teapot which is now in the Victoria and Albert Museum did not appear until circa 1670 and it was fashioned after the coffee pots of the day. These were tall, sometimes pear shaped and sometimes with sloping sides and the spout set fairly high up the pot, and fixed at right angles or at least at an acute angle. The handle was usually curved and as a rule a high-domed lid was fitted to the handle by a hinge.

This high design of the early coffee pots is reflected in a modified way in the tall Georgian teapots, and was so popular that the shape persisted, with some changes, for a good part of the eighteenth century.

Very few teapots in existence today go farther back than the time of Queen Anne and not many go back so far. Following the coffee pot these were octagonal or pyriform, but sometimes plain when they were decorated with floral scrolls; and this type was produced in Scotland in the first decade of the eighteenth century. The oval shaped teapot made its appearance a little later.

A practical innovation on those first Georgian teapots was the introduction of the wooden handle which was frequently of ivory but variations were of horn and ebony. It is surprising that so advantageous a feature was replaced later in the century by a silver handle matching the design of the pot. This looked attractive but the handle became agonizingly hot on the hand as soon as the tea was infused.

A protection against the heat was a small ivory or ebony knob attached to the lid. After being in disuse for some time the necessity to insulate the hand from the heat was recognized; therefore it is possible to acquire old teapots which have both the wooden handle and the wooden knob on the lid.

Small stands designed to follow the outline of the base of the teapot — usually circular or oval — were an inevitable accompaniment to the actual pot, and they prevented the heat from damaging the polished top of the table.

These useful little teapot stands were often quite

plain save for a crest or monogram in the center but others were decorated with scrolls or repousse. An old silver teapot with a small accompanying stand is a delightful asset to the tea table.

The serving of tea in the days of Queen Anne was a most gracious ritual, matching a gracious age. Boiling water was brought to the drawing room or boudoir by a servant, then the tea was infused by the hostess when it was placed over a spirit lamp — not too near or the silver would have melted. Then the mode changed and by the time George I sat on the throne the hot water was brought from the kitchen in a kettle and it stood over the spirit lamp to be brought again to the boil.

Where tea was to be served to a number of people urns were used. But the eighteenth-century urn is in less demand today than the teapot proper for the obvious reason that it demands more space than the average house can offer, and also for the somewhat drab reason that its usefulness does not match up to its decorative value. But where a niche can be found for it, it is suggestive of other days of elegant living.

Some beautiful silver urns were turned out by Robert Adam about 1760 and they continued to be made in comparatively large numbers until his death in 1792. His "vase" design, tapering to a circular foot, stands in a square base, supported by four ball feet, while a high tapering dome forms the lid and shaped handles circle above the urn in a graceful in-growing curve. The little tap which is turned to release the flow of tea is of ivory — sometimes of green ivory — and fan shaped.

Ornamentation on the urn was restrained. Occasionally there were decorations of scrolls and more often a beaded edge was frequent. Urns of the 1760–1790 period are the most desirable. Regency designs when the globular shape was in favor were less pleasing but they remained popular until about the middle of the nineteenth century.

The very existence of the urn presented a difficulty as it was not always easy to find a suitable place for it, and so a tiny urn table was created specially. The table was square with four slender legs which were either delicately turned or straight, with stretchers between, and fitted with a small movable slide just under the top of the table, to hold the cup while the tea was being poured out.

The urn table is an interesting survival but while it can still be picked up it is by no means common.

After the teapot and the tea urn were accepted pieces it was realized that a receptacle in which to keep the dry tea leaves when they were not in use was an essential part of the tea equipage. Hence the tea caddy. The first specimens were of fine porcelain and appear to have come from China and Japan in the late seventeenth century. Also from the East were caddies of lacquered wood and of ivory; and these were more practical than the porcelain and may occasionally be found.

The first English caddies were extremely plain; they were wooden boxes generally lined with tin foil after the fashion of the Chinese merchants who packed their tea like this when they imported it to the West. But with the fashion of serving and infusing tea in the drawing room this unadorned box was deemed uncouth and not quite in keeping with the elegant silver arrayed on the tea table.

Therefore the modest box was transformed into a more ambitious receptacle and the cabinet makers of the time set themselves to designing exquisite little caskets which would be in line not only with the beautiful teatime silver but also with the beautiful furniture which was gradually replacing the cumbersome pieces of the seventeenth century.

Early wooden caddies were made with curved tops and were known as tea trunks because of their resemblance to the luggage of the period. They were made in a variety of woods, such as rosewood, satinwood, walnut, fruit woods, tortoiseshell, and perhaps most popular of all, mahogany. As hostesses then liked to blend their own tea the cannisters were made with two compartments to contain the different brands of tea and these had flat, tight fitting lids which in later examples had small ivory knobs which acted as handles.

The reign of Queen Anne saw the introduction of the silver tea caddy, the epitome of beauty and luxury. It had a hinged lid often surmounted by a domed lid which was detachable and could be used for measuring the tea. An early design was tall, shaped like a bottle with a narrow neck, and this type was a direct copy of the first Oriental tea cannisters which had come from the East, and which were originally made of porcelain.

Such caddies resembled sugar casters in appear-

Unusual sexagonal tea caddy with painted panelled sides. (Courtesy John Bell)

Scottish silver tea caddy with lid and finely pierced feet. Made in Glasgow by Robert Gray in 1828. (Courtesy John Bell)

ance and were often chased and beaded. At this time tea was extremely expensive and consquently the containers were small. They may be found occasionally in pairs, to take different kinds of tea, and as an indication of their value, some caddies were fitted with a lock and key.

On octagonal cannisters the keyhole was placed slightly to one side if the position in the center interfered with the lines of decoration. Later caddies have a flat surface and are usually undecorated though there is sometimes a silver coin affixed to the lid, showing the head of George III. A beaded edge is usual. A rare find is a silver caddy with an engraved crest or monogram. This makes it a most desirable piece.

Some of the larger, plain boxes had in addition to the two compartments a small bowl in the center to take the sugar and this was often of wood with a painted Eastern design though sometimes it was of glass. The habit of having divisions in the caddies was continued until the early nineteenth century and afterwards and many of the smaller Regency examples have the two compartments.

Walnut caddies were popular in the reign of Queen Anne and so were in keeping with the walnut furniture then the fashionable wood. They were often inlaid with bands of other colored woods. It should be noted that until the end of the eighteenth century, and for some time afterwards, sugar as well as tea was a precious commodity, not to be used with abandon, and in the poorer homes its use was strictly limited to one day in the week, usually Sundays.

Tea caddies were produced in a host of different designs — circular boxes, attractive sarcophagus shapes, some like a high ink-bottle of ivory with arresting edges of ebony. Mother of pearl and ivory were both used as inlay. Those old cannisters are worth looking for.

Less usual was the glass caddy which first appeared about 1750. It was introduced by the glass workers of Bristol who were fast building up a reputation for their colored glass in rich reds and blues, and their glass caddies reached the heights of luxury and elegance. Clear glass was also used but the most desirable cannister was of blue Bristol intensely colorful and mounted in silver.

To protect them from accident those somewhat

frail containers were kept in a chest of shagreen, lined with velvet and decorated with silver.

To be complete the early caddy was fitted with two short handled little spoons for measuring out the tea, and these were made either of silver or ivory — but not many specimens have survived. This is strange as the silver spoons were made from circa 1750 until the end of the reign of George IV and were extremely attractive little pieces.

They were produced in various shapes, such as leaves, scoops, shovels and shells, or simply circular. Others were plain and pointed or had elaborate handles one of these taking the form of a serpent. Among the most decorative of the caddy spoons were those with the stem made of filigree. Sometimes the tiny bowl was also of filigree but this was less practical, though the pattern on the filigree was so fine that the tea leaves did not readily slip through.

Glass sugar boxes followed a similar design to the caddies but these had a hinged lid and silver finials. The design tended to be more square, almost cube shaped rather like an ink bottle on a solid base. They were often lavishly cut, flat diamonds being a frequent decoration. When Sheffield plate was introduced this metal was used in conjunction with glass instead of silver.

Some bottle shaped caddies were made of Bristol opaque white enamel glass. Those cannisters were most original being decorated after the manner of Chinese porcelain in Oriental colors, with gilt metal caps the tops of which were painted in enamel. This effect was intensified when the glass was held up to the light when it was creamy and translucent, much like porcelain.

By the mid-nineteenth century the importance of the luxurious caddy had dwindled considerably as by then tea had become more plentiful and it was no longer fashionable to have it infused in the drawing room. It was made in the kitchen, out of sight of the guests, and this did away with the need for the caddy which would be constantly on show when tea was served.

It is interesting to note that when tea-drinking was coming into its own as a social custom, in the early eighteenth century, small tables which could be easily moved about the room were practically non-existent. When the need for them was recog-

nized and the cabinet makers set about to remedy the lack of such tables, it became apparent that a small table was in itself insufficient so the tray also came into being.

Silver was the obvious metal for this very useful addition to the ceremony of drinking tea, and though some trays were square or oblong or even circular, it was the oval tray which was most successful; the reason was that it held a greater number of cups than the others. Its appearance too was more attractive.

Almost without exception all the trays of that period were beautiful. Sometimes they were ornamented with scrolls and foliage, while others were plain save for a crest. They rested on small ball feet and the handles were often of ebony, though the ivory type was fairly frequent; and sometimes a space through which the hands could be inserted was left at each end of the tray.

This latter arrangement perhaps makes the most desirable tray — the oval shape with a plain center surrounded by an elegant pierced gallery. The height of the gallery varies but in a large size it may be more than an inch deep and this lends unusual importance to the tray. It also acts as a support and prevents the china from falling off.

One of the disadvantages of a large silver tray containing the silver equipage must always be its weight and it is equally heavy when made of Sheffield plate. The trolley is the answer to this worry. There the weight is spread out and the effect enriches the silver appurtenances. But while nothing can surpass a silver tray in appearance, modern conditions forbid its use nowadays and a wooden tray is often employed in its place.

Some delightful wooden trays were turned out by the craftsmen of the eighteenth century, first in walnut and mahogany and later in the century in rosewood. The shapes of these trays were like those made in silver and the handles were usually fashioned of the same wood as the tray, or alternatively of ebony.

Sheraton's flair for producing beautiful pieces expressed itself in adding some inlay to the trays he made. This took the form of a center design fashioned from fruit woods in different colors, sometimes in a shell pattern which was very pleasing. There was also frequently a line of inlay edging the

Sheraton walnut tray with brass handles. (Courtesy John Bell)

protecting gallery which on some of the trays was unusually high. The obvious advantage of those eighteenth-century trays is that they can be used indefinitely without requiring attention save an occasional touch of polish. Many of them are in use today, their original charm quite undiminished.

There is another kind of tray which should not be ignored, the tray of papier mache. While they will not stand up to such hard treatment as either silver or wood, such trays with their gaily painted scenes and flowers and foliage are in considerable demand. Many are oval but others are of a shaped oblong design with elaborate shaping at the corners and the sides; and painted in bright colors which show up vividly against the black shiny background of the papier mache they are most decorative.

In Victorian times there was a great demand for all kinds of articles made in papier mache but for a good part of last century it fell from favor and was dismissed as a not too desirable relic. The ability to make articles from "mashed paper" is said to have been known to the Chinese centuries ago, and the secret was known also to the French early in the eighteenth century. It was not known in England however to any great extent, till Henry Clay of Birmingham took out a patent for its production in 1772.

About 1778 he took out another patent for decorating his pieces with mother of pearl. This he used particularly on flat surfaces such as tables and trays. This ornamentation was popular for many years. Clay used papier mache for other more ambitious purposes including varnished panels on coaches and on the sedan chairs of the time.

As the surface of the substance was inky black it was necessary to use very bright colors as a contrast, and his most effective treatment was by way of vividly painted floral schemes with gay tropical birds in flashing colors, along with mother of pearl ornament. He used it for small boxes, card cases and inkstands with some happy results. Papier mache is still fairly easy to find.

The salver, the smaller sister of the tray, is really the older of the two. It was known in the seventeenth century when it was used chiefly for serving wine, but it was not until the reign of Queen Anne when the serving of tea had become a friendly and social habit that the charms of the silver salver were fully recognized.

Early salvers were square in shape and had incurved corners, but a square salver was not convenient to take a number of circular wine glasses and by the middle of the century it had lost its appeal and gradually ceased to appear. There was still the occasional octagonal or oval type to be found but the circular salver had become the accepted type.

The most characteristic design had a narrow gallery or more often a shaped raised edge and there was often a shell or gadroon border. Beaded and reeded borders were also quite common. Salvers rested on tiny feet either bun shaped or claw and ball, the latter being more in demand.

It was usual to decorate the surface of the salver with scroll engravings, masks and vine leaves, or a shell ornament with the possible additional enrichment of a crest or monogram in the center. A plain surface in conjunction with a scalloped edge was one of the most pleasing designs. Salvers were made in a host of sizes, from the very minute tray which held only one cup or a single wine glass, to a much larger specimen almost as commodious as a real tray.

As has been suggested a very small amount of old English silver has survived. Much was lost when it was melted down to pay for the periodic wars in which the country was engaged, a certain amount was smuggled abroad, and a good deal was acquired by the Church when the monasteries were suppressed. In addition to all this wastage it was only natural that a certain proportion of silver should find its way to help the depleted royal coffers.

Apart from the financial loss however there is no great aesthetic deprivation to collectors because of the discovery of Sheffield plate which came on to the market at the time when it was most required, and the lovely old silver was copied with meticulous accuracy by the makers of the new plate. It was so well done that it was not possible to distinguish Sheffield from the genuine article without careful examination.

To most collectors the story of the origin of Sheffield plate is familiar. In 1742 a Sheffield cutler, Thomas Bolsover, or Boulsever, was repairing the handle of a knife which was composed partly of silver and partly of copper, when he discovered that when the two metals were fused the appearance of the exterior was exactly like silver.

From this exciting and accidental happening it was soon obvious that silver pieces lent themselves so well to the art of the cooper that it was not possible to determine the one from the other. The full extent of the invention was not at once apparent because the workers could not tell at that early stage whether the silver effect would last, or whether the copper might oust it from the surface and take the upper hand.

But time was on the side of Mr. Thomas Bolsover and one hopes he profited from the new plate. Gradually its enduring qualities became apparent. Apart from its modest cost, which was infinitely less than silver, it proved to be a most lucrative type of plate, and numerous companies were formed not only in Sheffield but in Birmingham also. Sheffield however gave its name to the production and so retained the honor of the discovery.

While Sheffield plate is generally accepted as the original method of applying silver to a base metal it is said that in ancient times both the cultured Egyptians and the Assyrians — and in later days the Romans — had also acquired the knowledge of fusing copper with silver. But they appear to have kept it to themselves and the English re-discovery by Bolsover seems to make its entrance to the Western world.

At first only small articles were turned out, such as buttons, buckles, patch boxes, snuff boxes, inkstands, egg cups, cruets, and knife handles, but gradually more ambitious products began to appear. Large trays, candlesticks and candelabra, teapots, coffee pots, urns, sugars and creams as well as toast racks, toddy ladles, and caddy spoons, to name only a few, all appeared in Sheffield plate. Indeed there were not many domestic articles which until then had been made only in wrought silver that were not now produced in the new silver plate which in appearance was exactly like solid silver.

One notable advantage of Sheffield was that from the first it was made in an age of craftsmen who were not only skilled, but who were working from designs which could not be improved upon. Therefore the impoverished aristocracy, who were in many cases replacing family heirlooms that had been lost or destroyed, were able to do so in the new plate, without fear that it should be suspect as not being the genuine article.

How much more would it have been appreciated could its owners have guessed that the articles so treated would remain in use with the appearance of the plate as good as ever and its value increased after constant use over a spell of about two centuries.

It seems unnecessary to say that the most desirable Sheffield was made in the eighteenth century which was truly the age of elegance. After the turn of the century designs in silver, as well as in furniture, began to deteriorate and the perfect taste that characterized the productions of the whole century affected also those of Sheffield plate. It followed the general trend and what had been restrained and beautiful now displayed an excess of ornament. Though plate was not affected so much as furniture the simple designs of the earlier Sheffield gave way to massive styles which had lost much of their grace.

Unfortunately very little of the old Sheffield plate was marked because of a law forbidding the marking by lettering of any article "made of metal or covered with silver, or upon any metal vessel or other thing made to look like silver." This law has made it difficult for collectors to identify the different periods as there was no assay mark. Many of the manufacturers in Sheffield and Birmingham tried, not unnaturally, to pass off their plate as sterling silver but this was circumvented by a law of prohibition.

It is not always fully realized that but for the invention of Sheffield plate in England many of the beautiful designs of sterling silver would have been lost to posterity. It was fortunate that when it was first made there was still a limited amount of silver in existence which could be copied exactly to give joy to coming generations including our own.

The appurtenances of the tea tray are not complete without the presence of small silver containers for sugar and cream. When they first appeared early in the eighteenth century they were termed cream pails and cream jugs and today they are among the daintiest little pieces likely to interest an aspiring collector.

Strictly speaking the pail did not belong to the tea tray. Pail and jug were used for different purposes and the cream jug appears to have been used on the dinner table, as well as at tea time, for serving cream over the sweet.

One of the earliest jugs was a short, low-bellied type with a shaped bow handle and a small lip resting on a circular reeded base. This was made in the time of the first George. But it is said there was even an earlier design which was somewhat similar, save that it had a straight neck, a simple bow handle, and no lip at all.

Some of the Queen Anne cream jugs were made in sets of three and authorities do not all agree on the reason for this. Specimens dating to the time of George II no longer had the ring base but were mounted on three elaborately cast feet. This does not seem to have been a satisfactory finish as the feet were not securely fixed, and were liable to become detached; later jugs made in the second half of the century show a plain ringed base or a slender stepped base. About 1790 there appeared a jug with a circular base which rested on a rounded foot and a short stem.

The silver cow cream jug came into fashion about 1767 but it was looked on more or less as a curio and there was no great demand for it in elegant homes.

Sugar basins or sugar baskets as they were sometimes called were not such early pieces as the cream jugs, and this is easy to understand when one examines a Queen Anne caddy which so often contained a compartment for the precious sugar. Small sugar basins did exist but according to some authorities a small bowl of an earlier date had been intended for some other purpose such as holding sweetmeats — or even for salt as at that time salt cellars tended to be large.

Early sugar basins had plain surfaces but in time they were embellished by embossed and fluted bodies. Pierced and fretted trellis work became a favorite decoration but this was not sufficient protection for the sugar and the idea was conceived of inserting a glass lining which fitted the interior of the basin. This prevented the sugar from running out. The lining was usually colored blue and the effect against the silver basket was most pleasing. Clear crystal was also used and sometimes ruby colored glass but the blue was the most popular.

One of the most charming sugar basins was like a deep bowl with piercing about an inch in depth surrounding the bowl a little way from the top. The basin had a slender circular handle which was very graceful. There was a short stem which stood on a slightly domed foot.

A flat band of silver often edged those old baskets and this gave scope to engravers who added a touch of extra ornamentation. Hexagonal and octagonal shapes were frequent as well as ovals and canoe shapes, and gradually, as the sugar basin became a part of the tea equipage in its own right, the designs began to follow those of the teapots, until finally when a tea service included the three pieces — teapot, sugar basins and cream jugs — they were designed as a matching set.

During the first part of the eighteenth century and for some decades afterward it was usual to have a lid on the basket, fitted with a finial so that it could be easily lifted. It has been suggested that remembering how expensive sugar was at that time, the lidded bowl was a reminder that its contents were not to be partaken of lightly.

A delightful design was oviform, finely chased and pierced and standing about five inches high with a delicate swing handle. This type was among the most elegant of sugar containers. Also most pleasing was the fluted sugar bowl which sometimes had ring handles and stood on tiny ball feet. Decorations increased considerably in the form of floral designs, festoons, and looped drapery, the kind of ornamentation used at the time on the backs of chairs.

Circular bowls were rarely produced but one sometimes comes across a conical basin resting on a circular foot, and having fluting and chasing and finished with a bale handle. An elaborate feature but one not often found is a lining of gilt instead of glass.

There does not seem to be any evidence as to whether butter dishes appeared with the tea equipage, but small dishes to hold butter have been known for a long time. According to an Inventory of the time "a butter cuppe of silver" was in the possession of one W. E. Grantham, who died in 1512. And though not many examples are seen today butter plates were made in the eighteenth century. They followed the silver patterns of the time including the sugar basins and cream jugs.

A glass lining was a frequent finish and the key pattern was often used in decorative bands across the outside of the dish. Some plates had shaped handles rising high from the sides and finishing low, on the body of the piece. The pierced gallery was a common form of decoration.

Some butter dishes were made with an accompanying stand which rested on four patterned feet, and occasionally there was a lid finished like the cover on the sugar basin with a delicate little knob. Other dishes had neither lid nor stand. Concerning butter plates it is of interest to note that when poorer members of the community went on a journey they took with them a specially made box to contain their own butter.

Of recent years examples of eighteenth-century butter plates either of silver or Sheffield plate have become extremely rare and are practically never mentioned in any list of old silverware offered for sale. One of its chief interests is that it was in use these many centuries ago; one of the earliest table refinements.

10

Candlesticks, Sconces, and Decorative Small Pieces

We are all so accustomed to adequate lighting in our homes nowadays that it is difficult to conceive just how our forebears coped with the awkwardness of long dark nights. With no gas and no electricity how did those industrious females — our ancestors — contrive to produce the fine stitchery which was essential for them to do in a machineless age? How were they able to read? How were the writers of precious manuscript able to turn out their perfect copperplate work?

In the seventeenth century movable lanterns and candlesticks with screens, when this was necessary, were usual in modest homes as they could be easily carried about. In larger establishments this was augmented by sconces which were attached to the walls. Samuel Johnson defined the word "sconce" as "a punsile candlestick generally with a looking glass behind to reflect the light." The term "girandole," a word derived from the Italian, embraces both candlesticks and fixed wall brackets which give light.

In the great manor houses of medieval days sconces fitted with back plates were known, and a jewelled example now in the Louvre, belonged to Catherine de Medici. In England during the seventeenth century wall plates were made of silver and gilt but earlier examples were of earthenware. By the end of the century metal was generally used

for sconces, because, it is believed, pewter or brass helped to give added reflection when the candle was lit. The actual plate was plain or flat or it had a convex center with embossed ornament.

The helpful Samuel Pepys had a word about sconces. In 1692 he recorded in his Diary that he "spent most of the morning hanging up pictures, and seeing how my pewter sconces that I have bought, well become my stayres and entry." Brass sconces were decorative and were often hung by gold or yellow silk cords fitted with a tassel; and silver or silver gilt sconces made in numerous patterns were fashionable about the time of the Restoration.

These however were not an innovation, as in Elizabethan times silver sconces were hung on the walls of Hampton Court Palace, and "four large hanging wall candlesticks" were listed in the plate belonging to Charles I in the Tower of London and it may be taken as possible that while there is no special mention of sconces in the Inventory of Henry VIII, he probably possessed several lots to match his silver candlesticks of which he "had a great many" decorating his palaces.

Some sconces with a flat back plate had a projecting tray on which the candle holder was set. These were popular in the latter decades of the seventeenth century and as the holder was intended to collect the grease from the candles it was a type often made in the base metals.

About the time of the Restoration, after his return from France, Charles II had some elaborate sconces made in brass, with such fine ornamentation that they surpassed many silver specimens. Sometimes they were designed in the form of an arm or a hand. Other elegant sconces were of blue and white enamel and at the turn of the century when glass was reaching its height of popularity it became the mode to have glass sconces set in a metal frame.

It was rather earlier than this, circa 1660, that the word girandole began to be found in the French Royal Inventories. Ralph Edwards says, "This name was given at first to candelabra in which the arms were made so as to form a cone of light." Many of the girandoles so described in the gay salons of Versailles were probably movable candelabra. When they were copied by the English they were made in wood as well as in metal.

The fashion for having back plates or reflectors of looking glass is accentuated when in the Council Chamber of Kensington Palace several were stated to be old, when the Inventory was drawn up in 1697. In the early eighteenth century a popular type of sconce had a narrow back plate of bevelled glass, straight or scalloped, and ornamented with a diamond cut pattern. Another design having the plate set in the wood was listed in the Royal Accounts.

Sconces of varying design remained in favor throughout the eighteenth century — a most charming fashion. In the reign of George I they were of carved and gilt wood which gave no reflection, and so it was modish during this period to have candle brackets surmounted by glass globes to add to the general lighting. By the middle of the century sconces were found in gilt frames while others were of glass.

The cabinet maker of the day recognized the aesthetic appeal of candlelight placed in a fine setting, and Robert Adam was one of those who designed some sconces to tone with his mirrors and with the plaster wall ornamentation. Hepplewhite, and later in the century Sheraton, also made some delightful glass girandoles fitted with candles and made to be hung on the wall.

The eighteenth century produced another type of wall lighting. This was used in conjunction with hanging mirrors when candle branches, usually of brass, were attached to the bottom of the frame to reflect the light. Chippendale liked this form of lighting very much and it is found in many of his beautiful perpendicular mirrors where it was fixed to the two lower corners of the frame.

In addition to improving the general lighting effects those sconces also contributed something to the heat of the rooms in which they were placed. In large and very often drafty establishments this was no mean feat and must have been a most welcome asset.

Mirrors with candle attachments persisted into the furnishing schemes of the nineteenth century and they were still popular in Regency days; they extended their charm to the small convex gilt studded mirror which had appeared a short time before. About the end of the eighteenth century wall lights of cut glass were in favor and with faceted branches and festoons of drops glittering in the glass these were extremely effective.

To a considerable extent it was the combined employment of glass with a naked flame which added so much to the popularity of glass, and this persisted in spite of the Excise Duty which was imposed on it in 1745. It was looked on as patriotic to encourage this peculiarly English industry.

The next progressive step in lighting was the chandelier or hanging candlestick as it was also called. This can be traced back to the glass wall lights the first of which were made circa 1760 at Stourbridge. It is said that the first chandelier produced there was kept near the factory for many years as a show piece.

Nothing so exciting as those initial chandeliers had previously appeared to delight the eyes. Designs varied but by the beginning of the nineteenth century glass drops set closely together were mounted on a frame work, usually of metal, which was almost hidden by the tightly knit arrangement of the drops shaped like a glittering bowl.

At Carlton House King George III had a great lustre of glass and ormolu which was described as looking like a shower of diamonds and was said to have cost between £2,000 and £3,000. What a sight those lustres must have been and how gay and lovely the scene when men and women, painted and powdered and bewigged, danced beneath the flashing lights.

Eighteenth-century hanging mirrors are still plentiful but those possessing the brass branches are not so often found. This is because the looking glass as such was both decorative and useful, and was cared for by its owners, while the candle attachments were considered superfluous after candles went out of fashion, and were discarded.

Lighting supplied by chandeliers and sconces was immovable and gave the background lighting to the room. But this general light did not meet every need; thus when local lights were required for sewing or reading these were given by candlesticks, and also by candelabra, which held a number of candles and which could be placed at a convenient height and distance for such occupations.

Furniture designers, ever quick to follow a lead, gave their attention to the necessity for improved movable lighting. Contemporary small writing desks, escritoires and card tables made provision for the candles by fitting a slide or pull-out attachments, on which candles could stand, on many of the pieces they were making.

It was discovered that when a candle was used on a polished surface of wood the reflection of the flame helped to increase the illusion of light, and it is possible that this was one of the reasons for the candlelit, highly polished dinner tables which were so much in vogue, as well as for the candles fitted to hanging mirrors which also seemed to augment the illumination of the room.

Those lights already mentioned, sconces and chandeliers, tall branched and silver candelabra, were, however, the kind used in the homes of the aristocracy and the wealthy, and were rarely if ever seen in more modest dwellings. They used instead brass and pewter and wood.

Silver sconces and candlesticks were usual forms of lighting by the more affluent classes and it is unfortunate that because of the custom of discarding or breaking up old plate, when it was damaged or seemed out of date, few examples now exist.

The manufacture of sconces suffered a setback at the time of the introduction of the French rococo style when a number of craftsmen ceased to have an interest in their production. These included the japanners, the goldsmiths, and the cabinet makers, but not the brass worker who made cast brass sconces after the French designs and who turned out much beautiful brass work. Those foundry specimens were so much liked that they continued to be made in the Regency period.

It has been said that furniture throughout the ages has come into being as and because it was required. All furniture was designed to suit the period in which it was to be used. This was obvious about the beginning of the nineteenth century when there was a marked change in the domestic lighting of rooms. With the arrival of gas as a means of lighting, bureaux and gaming tables were no longer designed to have a slide for candlesticks.

The bureau bookcase too was now constructed without provision in the interior for candlesticks, and the same was true regarding other pieces where a candle had formerly been essential. Even before gas lighting became common there was an inclination to dispense with candles for localized purposes because of the light given by the chandeliers and wall sconces. Marble was sometimes used for these instead of glass and sometimes blue john, mounted with gilded metal but nothing was so pleasing as the cut glass; nothing enhanced those modish assemblies so much as the gleam of the cut glass chandeliers.

For local lighting — sewing and the like — candle stands were popular in the reign of Charles II. These took the form of a plain or spiral baluster with a circular or octagonal top resting on a tripod base. Walnut was the wood most frequently used though elm stands were also made. In the time of William and Mary several stands were of walnut with an inlay of olive wood and a decade or two later gilt candle stands were often used at large receptions.

By the middle of the century the number of candlesticks had very much increased and different woods and styles were used. Chippendale used mahogany and his designs of stands, that were carved and gilded and sometimes painted as well, made of this simple piece a most elegant holder for candles and candelabra. In some of his stands the candelabrum formed an actual part of the structure while others supported twisted branches of wrought iron. Candle stands are not easy to acquire but small stands originally intended to hold plants some of them made in the nineteenth century are very pleasing indeed.

In Scotland the candle stand was of wrought iron and was called the puirman. This is a smallish tripod type standing on a column of twisted iron with three twisted legs splaying at the floor. At the top it is fitted with a branched fixture which takes one or two—sometimes three — candles — and the effect is very artistic.

It is interesting to trace the growth of the candlestick. It was introduced into England after the early rushlight which was a product of country smiths. In those days the candles were stuck on spikes to keep them steady. When the candlesticks came on the scene, the next improvement was to have a sliding holder so that the height of the candle might be regulated.

It gradually became fashionable to place candlesticks on dining tables and also on tables near to which one was reading or sewing. Then one had to have a candle to light one to bed and this resulted in one of the most graceful shapes — the small neat saucer shaped chamber candlestick. In silver this is perhaps the most delectable of all sticks for display purposes and it has a practical finish — a small snuffer fixed to the edge of the tray. In the days when candlesticks were laid out on the hall for people about to retire there must always have been sufficient space for the little chamber candlestick.

Another popular stick was the pillar shape. Its tall columns were reeded and mounted on a square, slightly stepped base which was very firm and solid and admirable for use on a dining table. These two designs were the most popular type in England for many years.

Then came the candle lamp. Oil had now very largely superseded the candle and the appearance of oil lighting was a great advancement as candles of those early days gave but a glimmer of light which left much to be desired. The molding of candles was at one time a domestic duty as they were made from various fats which had accumulated in the kitchen in the course of cookery.

When the candles were made they were hung up by their wicks in bunches till they were required by the household. Other which were needed for immediate use were stowed away in candle boxes. Considering the inadequacy of the home-made candle it is surprising that it was not until the eighteenth century that any serious attempt seems to have been made to replace it by the oil lamp.

As with the furniture of the period it was fortunate that candle lamps were introduced at a time when excellence of design and skill in craftsmanship were at their height of perfection. Consequently for those early specimens the workers copied some of the beautiful bronze lamps of ancient Greece and Rome and reproduced them in brass and copper. In Victorian times some such lamps were still in use in country districts and while they are now rare they may still be had in out of the way areas.

In the eighteenth century street lighting was practically non-existent and portable lanterns for use in town and country were a necessity. For urban use the lantern was made of horn which was a light weight material to carry around. Those in the country were of iron and tin and it is notable that there is a pronounced similarity between the lanterns of two hundred years ago and the modern decorative type on sale today.

Once oil lamps became the rule one might have thought that the candle would be ousted but this was not so. This gentle illumination, so becoming to the skin, persisted in all classes of society for generations. Collectors sometimes complain about the difficulty in finding an exact pair of candlesticks, but it is surprising that so many single sticks have survived and in a good state of preservation. This applies particularly to those made in silver as so many were destroyed throughout the various periods for different reasons.

The very early candlesticks were of treene — wood — or of pewter or horn or leather, with a very small proportion in silver or silver gilt. In spite of its being so soft a metal pewter was possibly the most popular but it was readily destroyed by heat and examples in mint condition are not easy to find. Matching pairs are extremely rare.

Brass candlesticks had more lasting qualities than pewter and they were in constant demand being used in church and home alike. One of the most decorative is the high standing church piece, the pricket type of candlestick. It is not fitted with a socket and the candle is kept in an upright position by means of a sharp iron pin, on which it is impinged. The great advantage of this 'stick is that without the confining influence of a socket, candles of different lengths can be used.

While it is essentially a church piece the design was also produced in a smaller size for domestic purposes. It is admirable for a hall. Other domestic candlesticks were fitted at the base with a slender rod of iron which could be pushed right up the hollow stem reaching to the candle, and extending its life. This was a common adjunct in seventeenth-century candles.

Few brass candlesticks in general use are older than the early seventeenth century. At that time they were shaped like an upturned drinking cup, of the chalice type, with addition of a tubular socket. In later specimens the cup is merged into a tray which is so fashioned that it catches the wax or grease as it drips down the column. On Jacobean brass candlesticks a small inverted grease tray is usually fixed above the base — in this case the base is square with a circular or fluted column — and this adds to the general appearance.

Towards the end of the reign of Charles II cast baluster stems with hammered bases were beginning to be seen and at the beginning of the eighteenth century when designs were smaller and lighter the grease tray was no longer used.

In the eighteenth century candlesticks were made with a solid base which was heavily weighted, so that in that gaming age it would not be readily knocked over from the card table. A novelty introduced in Queen Anne's time and in use for some decades afterwards was the movable nozzle. Baluster stems were also common and the sticks stood firmly on a broad base.

Other candlesticks had a high domed foot closely resembling the base of the drinking and sweetmeat glasses of the period and this was a very graceful design. As brass candlesticks were not marked it is not possible to state accurately their age, and the collector is guided by the design and some features which cannot be simulated on modern sticks. Brass candlesticks were made in pairs but over the years one may become damaged or lost and it is easier to pick up single specimens without their neighbor.

Among the smaller brass pieces which should not be overlooked by the collector are horse brasses or horse jewellery as it is sometimes more piquantly called. These are very old; it is said the origin goes back about two thousand years. The term horse brasses is given to the small decorative brass discs which adorned the magnificent draught horses so long as they were in use.

Legend has it that the Roman occupiers of Britain between 50 A.D. and 410 A.D. instituted the custom of enriching leather harnesses of the horses with bronze amulets, and those amulets bore a strong likeness to the horse brasses which made their reappearance in England at the time of the coronation of Queen Victoria. Limited quantities have been made ever since.

The idea of horse brasses originated with the Moors who believed that if the horses wore those glittering sun brasses they would be guarded from the evil eye. The habit still persists at horse shows and fairs in remote areas. Brasses were used lavishly. As many as forty or fifty might be worn by a horse in full dress, while on ordinary occasions there might be two ear brasses, ten on the martingale, and possibly three suspended from the straps on each shoulder.

Early brasses were chiefly sun flashes, and a crescent design with incurving horns and a pair of wings extending outward. A personal note was struck when brasses were issued as souvenirs. About the time of Queen Victoria's succession makers issued brasses that had some connection with the purchaser's trade, and these were termed occupational brasses. A man with a crook indicated a shepherd, a man with a horse pointed to a ploughman, while a wagoner with his whip was meant for a farm worker. There were also commemorative brasses including one of Victoria herself. Horse shoes were naturally used as a symbol of good luck.

Horse brasses can be most attractively displayed. One suggestion is to thread a number of them on a long strip of scarlet or black leather and hang them on a doorway or on the wall of a cream or white painted room. Or again they make wonderful door handles, or bedroom knockers, and they are effective when placed against panelling — a panelled oak wall is an excellent background.

A delightful small piece for a bedroom or sitting room is the sampler, so called because at first it was an "exampler" or a sample to be copied. The sampler is essentially an English piece and was mentioned in literature before 1500, though one of the earliest known specimens is dated 1643. It forms a most intimate link between past and present, as it was such a family piece, a duty performed by little girls when they were learning to sew.

It was known in the time of Shakespeare. In *Midsummer Night's Dream* Helen says, "We, Hermia, like two artificial gods, have with our needles created both a flower, both on one sampler sitting on one cushion." Another quotation, from *Titus Andronicus,* is, "Fair Philomel she but lost her tongue and in a tedious sampler sewed her mind."

In an earlier day John Skelton, born in the latter years of the fifteenth century, became Poet Laureate of England and spoke of "the sampler to sew on, the lacis to embraid." The earliest known reference to samplers is in the Inventory of Queen Elizabeth I, and it was during the late sixteenth and early seventeenth centuries that the designing and making of samplers reached their heyday. Pursuits at that time were limited and needlework of all kinds was one of the chief occupations of women of all ages and classes.

A sampler was not a piece of work which could be completed in a week or two. Depending on the elaboration of the design this might take a considerable time to accomplish. As is revealed from some samplers which give the dates of beginning and ending this piece of work might occupy the young sewer for several months or even several years.

Although generally designs have altered considerably down through the years, the basic designs have remained the same. Those made in the seventeenth century were mostly floral and geometrical. Pansies, honeysuckle, strawberries and lillies were some of the flowers used. The acorn was sometimes used as a way of commemorating the Boscobel Oak under whose branches Charles II sheltered in 1651.

The actual shape of the sampler varied. Nearly all examples made prior to the eighteenth century were long and narrow and were from six to eight inches wide. Very large ones might be as long as three feet. They were worked on bleached or unbleached linen with embroidery in white or colored silk and an occasional metal thread.

Eighteenth-century designs showed a distinct change. About the end of the seventeenth century samplers tended to be shorter and narrower and colors were more vivid than they had yet been in accordance with the gay century just beginning. With the increasing interest in learning the alphabet was taking on a new importance and the "letters" as well as the numbers began to predominate on the samplers of that era.

A pictorial effect was achieved by a strip of landscape or a small square house, conventional in design with stiff little trees and pots of flowers surrounding it. It was usual too for the seamstress to insert her name and the date of her birth, and there were also samples of the different stitches which the child had been taught.

About 1725 a loose coarse woollen background came into fashion instead of the earlier linen but by the end of the century there was a reversal of taste and linen was again popular. A new note in the last decades of the eighteenth century was the map sampler, showing the village or hamlet where the young embroideress had been brought up.

The framing of samplers deserves some attention as an old sampler placed in a modern frame loses some of its appeal. Fortunately old frames can still be picked up at prices not too exorbitant. Choose if possible a wood which was popular when the sampler was made: walnut for early specimens, mahogany for the eighteenth and ninteenth centuries and rosewood for those that were sewn in the Regency period.

Old prints are delightful articles to collect and have something of the appeal of the sampler, though the print is a comparatively young antique. Bird and floral prints were produced as early as the eighteenth century and some a little earlier than that, but the nineteenth century was the time when prints appeared in quantity.

Any prints bought today should be in color. There is little or no demand for the black and white type. The Baxter print is best known and is extremely charming. It is also the most expensive. George Baxter was the son of a well-known printer and publisher, and he was born at Lewes in Sussex in 1804. Early in his life he showed his artistic leanings and as a young man he spent a good deal of his leisure time in the practice of color printing. He is believed to have been inspired by the engraver Thomas Benick, a contemporary of his —

1753–1828 — who produced many beautiful bird prints.

Baxter's first work which he published in 1830, when he was still in his twenties, was in color. He called it Butterflies. It was very skilfully executed and he was the first to bring to the homes of the people artistic reproductions of all kinds of paintings, both historic and topical.

He was a most conscientious worker and in addition to his being a master of his craft he was also an artist of no mean merit. Every detail of his work received his own personal supervision and this, added to his artistic temperament, resulted in prints of such excellence that he led the field completely.

The subjects used by Baxter are legion. From the reproduction of landscapes he moved to copying popular paintings representing some contemporary happening, such as the coronation of Queen Victoria, the opening of her first Parliament, and the great industrial exhibitions in Hyde Park and at Sydenham. He also reproduced paintings of famous people, such as Maria Chubb, wife of Charles Chubb the famous locksmith; and a portrait of the Duke of Wellington was published in 1852, the year of his death.

Baxter's art suffered from the introduction of the colored lithograph and also by the growth of photography, both processes being much cheaper and faster to produce than Baxter's own works. After his many years of toil he was beaten by the march of time and he was forced into bankruptcy in 1864. In this year, his career resembles that of Thomas Sheraton the famous cabinet maker who himself created so much beauty for others to enjoy yet died a poor and broken man.

For anyone anxious to acquire some old prints it is wise to make sure that the copy is clean and unfaded, not torn and not creased, and with coloring undamaged. The approximate date of a Baxter print can be discovered from the date on the print. If prints are found in bound volumes the book should be carefully preserved intact and not exposed to strong sunlight.

There is a certain vogue just now for collecting door knockers, and on an old house these are most charming. Authorities differ in their opinions regarding the beginning of the door knocker. Some people date it as early as the fourteenth century, while others place it much later, but while in some shape or other the knocker or bell is now an essential of modern domestic equipment at the entrance to a house or flat, it does not appear to have been in use until the seventeenth century.

Until that time traffic was limited and one presumes that front doors were kept in a perpetual state of "openness" and no permanent fixture was needed to draw attention to guests who had arrived unexpectedly on the doorstep.

Early knockers were of iron and in the eighteenth century iron was still used, but it was shaped by casting instead of being wrought. The rapper portion was made in the form of a ring — circular, oval or shaped — while the design of the back plate was usually fashioned like a head. The design of a very early knocker might consist of a winged dragon forming the hammer against a grotesque back plate The heads of all kinds of animals such as a lion, a horse or a goat, a satyrs's mask, a sphinxes head, a Medusa and caryatid figures, all appeared on those knockers.

By the eighteenth century styles were modest but they still tended to be large, for even in quite small dwellings of that time the front door was big and heavy and a knocker light in weight would not have been heard throughout the house. Early knockers were of iron and therefore of no intrinsic value. Consequently little care was taken of them and the survivors are few. But they do exist and are intriguing to look for.

Some Georgian rappers are charming with good designs and a sale of the contents of an old country house may produce one or two. A fairly common knocker in the Adam tradition sometimes had the back plate in the shape of an urn with a graceful semi-circular ring as rapper. Another design of about the same period might have the rapper in the form of an Egyptian mummy.

Country door knockers were sometimes made in the form of a bird such as a woodpecker. In the nineteenth century, shapes varied a good deal and those made about 1820 were of malleable cast iron which was invented at the beginning of the century. For a long time iron continued to be the most popular material for the knocker and while it has been replaced by the more decorative brass knocker the iron knocker is still found on main doors as well as on back doors.

11

Card Tables

The gaming or games table — what is now called the card table — came into its own in the gay days of the eighteenth century when gaming and gambling parties had become the rage as a nightly diversion for the leisured upper classes. Card games had been popular in England for several centuries and as early as the reign of the first Elizabeth an oak table intended for backgammon and draughts had been produced. It was a very solid piece with a double folding top, very similar to that in use about a couple of centuries later.

In the late seventeenth century when Charles II was influencing domestic taste by encouraging the production of much beautiful furniture some lovely walnut games tables appeared. They were probably the first small tables made specifically for card playing — apart from the "shove" table or shovelboard table which was much bigger and had been used for the game of shovel board by Henry VIII. Because they were not made in any great numbers few of them exist today.

The card table in the style which we know it was made at first with leaves which pulled open in the manner of the gate-leg table with the movable leg. Sometimes it had two legs which swung round to support the hinged leaves. While some of those early tables were of oak, by the time Queen Anne had succeeded to the English throne the majority were either of walnut or of oak with a walnut veneer. They were thus less cumbersome than oak and were more elegant as a drawing room piece.

The card table most typical of the early eighteen hundreds was of walnut, with a circular folding top, and it had slender cabriole legs ending in hoof feet or in claw and ball feet. The edges of those tables were rounded but had projecting corners shaped as segments of a circle, and when the table was opened up there were little receptacles on the surface, which was slightly sunk to take them, on which the candlesticks rested. In addition to the little receptacles for candlesticks, some tables had little scooped recesses alongside; these were intended for the players' counters or coins.

There was little carving on the legs of the early tables and while cabriole was the most favored design there was the occasional table which had straight legs and bun feet. Mahogany, it will be remembered, was not used for furniture in England to any extent until about 1715 just after George I had succeeded Anne on the throne.

A feature of the Queen Anne games table was the beautifully shaped top made by the corner recesses, and which was revealed when the flap was folded back. There was a little carving at the knees and on the hoof feet — all very restrained and elegant. Gradually carving became more emphatic especially as a decoration on the cabriole legs, when the most common enrichment was the shell.

The claw and ball feet began to be seen about 1700 or possibly a little earlier and it made a satisfactory finish to the legs of tables and of chairs also. Until about the middle of the century it was extremely popular and cabinet makers experimented with the various birds from which to produce the claw. The eagle was popular and carving of the feet began to be more lavish. Card tables which were finished with the plainer pad foot were, however, more distinctive.

When mahogany tables were made the wood demanded a treatment slightly different from that used on the oak and walnut, but the designs, having proved their usefulness, remained much the same. The new wood lent itself to the bolder carving which was beginning to show itself. Carved masks and shells enriched the knees and open scroll carving sometimes extended beyond the knees.

A point of interest to the collector is that although in the early tables the recesses for candlesticks were circular they were now made square to accommodate a change in the design of the candlesticks.

Those recesses, though appearing frequently, were not always present. Sometimes in their place there was a small shaped sliding panel of matching walnut, which swung out from beneath the table and this had a fitment for the candlestick. When not in use this could easily be slid back again.

As the century advanced card tables developed on more severe lines. But about 1760 at the beginning of the reign of George III Chippendale made some delightful games tables, which though they were made of mahogany echoed those of Queen Anne's day. The carving round the angular top and at the lower edge of the apron, the grace of the cabriole leg (though the cabriole leg was more modified than it had been), and the knee carving, also the small hoof feet, all these points made it an outstanding piece.

It differed from the early types in that apart from the carved edge on the rectangular top the line was unbroken with no interruptions for candlesticks or for money. As the interior of such tables was of wood — not the most suitable surface for card playing — the top was covered with green cloth. Baize

was the workaday material used on tables which were in nightly use but in better-class homes this was replaced by a cover of finer stuff.

Fine wool tapestry which was already very much in demand for Queen Anne chairs and stools was often repeated in petit point on the games table. A top like this, undamaged, is now hard to find but now and again a lovely old cover crops up, the colors muted and faded, but still pleasing. Other covers were made of linen delicately embroidered with hearts, spades, etc., sewn at each corner, and sometimes a monogram. Velvet was another favorite covering.

A practical touch was that when tables were fitted with scooped-out hollows for the candlesticks, the covers were not made to extend to the edge of the table. This prevented the recesses from being spotted by candle grease which could not be readily removed from such fine fabrics as velvet or tapestry whereas any damage could be easily cleaned from the bare wood.

Later in the century the semi-circular table was in popular demand. This of course was a circle when the flap was folded back and the table opened up. In the mahogany semi-circular type a small drawer for the counters is fitted under the framing, and there were sometimes pull-out trays to hold the candlesticks. Those were inlaid or covered in silk.

Games tables which were more strictly for gaming, made circa 1770, were occasionally made in the shape of a refectory table, long and narrow. This made the table more resistant and prevented its tilting if someone leaned on it suddenly. For further protection tables of this kind might have a pierced metal gallery and this prevented the contents — glasses, decanters, and possibly candlesticks — from being knocked to the floor.

Although mahogany began to be used shortly after the second decade of the century and continued indefinitely from that time on, numerous card tables were still being produced in walnut, and as already mentioned, a delightful finish to the rectangular table was an edging of fine carving which bordered the top and the underframing. Chippendale often finished his card tables — and other tables also — in this way.

The entry date of mahogany into the domestic scene in England is always of interest and in view of the fact that authorities hold different opinions regarding this, it is intriguing to discover from historical data the approximate date when mahogany furniture began to be used in England.

In a list of goods to be sold and advertised in the *Daily Courant* of 15th November 1723 there is mention of mahogany dining tables, and a further advertisement in the *Daily Journal* of 3rd December 1724 states, "to be sold by auction . . . tables of several sorts, both wallnutt tree and mahogany, and mahogany lanthorns for halls and stair cases." On June 6, 1727, the *Daily Post* includes in a sale of Furniture belonging to a Fellow of the College of Surgeons, "mahogany bookcases, burows (bureaux one presumes) tables, etc."

From about that time on mahogany furniture is often mentioned along with that of "Wallnutt tree." A piece of contemporary evidence whose authenticity cannot be doubted comes from the Royal Household accounts when in 1724 there is an Invoice of John Gumley and Moore, in which the following items are listed: "four wallnutt trees & two mahogany desart tables upon brass wheels, £31–10; two mahogany cloths chests £16; a mahogany supping table £4."

Apparently the first mention of a royal gaming table came in 1728 when Elizabeth Gumley and William Turing, cabinet makers, supplied "for his Majesties" service at Kensington a large mahogany table for play, £4. About the same time an oval "mahogany" table was made for Princess Mary at a cost of £2–10.

It is an interesting point that those household pieces made in the first part of the eighteenth century consisted almost entirely of tables. They were astonishingly assorted: dressing, night, dining, writing, play (games), music, and breakfast tables to mention only a few. These were listed in the Royal Household accounts between 1729 and 1733, and it was not until the appearance of the next batch of accounts that a wider selection of mahogany articles appeared.

This is partly explained by the many new pieces of furniture which the more lavish circumstances of the day had suggested and which the skilled cabinet makers were only too anxious to produce. Thus chests of drawers, bureaux, chairs, cabinets and bookcases were made to delight the prosperous citizens who had ordered them. What an exciting time it must have been in which to choose furniture for one's home.

According to statistics of imports, mahogany began to be imported from Jamaica into England in small but increasing quantities from about 1715 on. To begin with the output was confined mainly to small pieces. The amount of wood which was arriving was so limited that for some years there was not sufficient wood to supply the eager demands of the cabinet makers who were naturally anxious to stock up with the new wood.

This question of supply and demand resulted in an increase of workmen, and small tables were made in considerable quantities not only by the well-known London cabinet makers and joiners who lived near at hand, but by other craftsmen, some of them untrained, who lived by the sea or close enough to ports where the mahogany was being landed to benefit by their circumstances.

The fact that emphasis was placed on the making of the small pieces encouraged the manufacture of the card tables, and from the early years of the eighteenth century competent workmen were turning out attractive examples. Finely made tables were produced by all the eminent cabinet makers including Chippendale, Hepplewhite and later on by Sheraton, and specimens are still comparatively easy to find.

By the middle of the century the cabriole leg had been ousted by the straight leg. This was usually tapered and ended in a spade foot. Mahogany was the wood of that period but many walnut gaming tables persisted as the cabinet makers recognized the decorative qualities of the wood.

Towards the end of the century when Sheraton had joined the select band of craftsmen he displayed his liking for originality and also his love of color by making tables of mahogany and decorating them with satinwood; and he introduced a new note by making an inlay pattern in the center of the tables of different woods. This resulted in a gay design of varied colors, which was most effective. Sheraton used ebony as a typical finish.

Many collectors search for gaming tables today who have no intention of using them for this purpose, as the folding card table makes an excellent dining table in a small household. It is equally useful for this purpose whether it is round or rectangular, though the accommodation provided by the circular table is more ample.

Among the many little tables made by Chippendale were some delightful rectangular mahogany tables, and while those were originally meant for casual use in the hall they make ideal card tables particularly those with a double folding top which is square when it is opened up. The legs in those tables were always straight and if they were not carved they were reeded. Sometimes they were tapered but this was less frequent than a straight leg the same width all the way down, but which was so well proportioned that even when it was thick it was still pleasing.

Some of those rectangular tables show distinct traces of the Chinese Chippendale influence, notably in the pierced frets between carved legs and in the under framing.

Of the smaller gaming tables one of the most pleasing is the half moon or D-end design with the double top which can be opened up by means of a folding leg which is swung round to support the extra leaf. This table is invariably found in mahogany. Its legs may be straight and slightly tapered or made in the form of a modified cabriole. This makes a table which is exactly right in size for card playing and it is frequently copied today.

The real D-end table should also be considered. This originally was part of the large dining table in common use in the eighteeenth century. It could be made into a really large table by means of additional "leaves" and by the two D-ends. These were semi-circular pieces which were fitted by means of brass clasps to the ends of the table and when they are placed together they form an extremely attractive dining table suitable for today's requirements.

Though rather large for a card table in the usual sense those D-ends vary in size and sometimes they can act very well in this capacity. They are however more useful in the twentieth century as a complete dining table when the two are placed together to form a circle. Used in this way they can seat an unexpectedly large number of people. When placed in different rooms their decorative value is considerable.

In the latter decades of the eighteenth century a host of attractive rectangular tables, eminently suitable for card playing, appeared perhaps as a result of the success of the earlier tables of this type introduced by Chippendale. They hardly resembled the Chippendale table at all save that they were both made of mahogany, and in the same rectangular shape.

The design of this later table was almost severe. Reeded along the edge of the top they had a long shallow drawer across the front fitted with circular brasses. Frankly, as it doesn't have a double top, this table is not broad enough for a card table. Its slender legs tapering to the floor give it a delicate air and suggest its suitability as a dressing table in a guest room, or as a dining table for one person. This is the kind of table for which there is always a use and it is a delightful acquisition.

One of the earliest mahogany tables was the gate-leg having its circular top mounted on a carved pillar which ended in three splayed legs. To emphasize the design when they were first made they were called realistically "a table on a pillar." Such a table was supplied to the Royal Household of George I in 1729 for the modest sum of £1-15.

This design seemed to have been designed specially for mahogany and unlike the gate-leg table it had never been produced in oak. The new eighteenth century mahogany pieces were first planned with the wealthy classes in mind but in quite a short time they were also being made in plainer designs, more in keeping for those who were less well-to-do. Any collector who is interested in such a table should view with some suspicion any carving which may adorn it, as some of the furniture fakers of a later day applied carving in the hope that it would increase the value.

It was from the tripod that the dumb waiter first emanated in the reign of George I, circa 1726. The dumb waiter consisted of a two- three- or four-tiered stand which was fixed to a tripod base and stood on brass casters. This piece seems to have been made of mahogany always. To avoid a clumsy appearance the circular trays of the waiter had to be made from one piece of very thin wood which yet had to be strong enough to stand up to daily use without twisting.

Adam made an unusual little games table in the Pembroke style. The main body was of satinwood with a touch of inlay on the top and an edging of ebony, and when it was opened up it was a small square very suitable for card playing. The small drawer was inlaid and the legs were very slender and finished in spade feet.

About the end of the eighteenth century or possibly a little later a desirable little table appeared. It was called a Regency-and-games table. In spite of its name it was rectangular in shape and seated two players not four. The side supports were reeded and curved inwards to meet the stretcher and beneath these were other reeded stretchers curving outward in Regency fashion. Those were mounted on brass casters which by that time had superseded the leather wheeled type of the last decades of the eighteenth century.

A shallow drawer seemed to stretch across the apron front but this was really a sham, though in the center there was a small lock and key. The apron front was curved and very slightly shaped towards the center which lent a certain grace to the general effect as did the center cross stretcher which was turned and very slender.

This small card table is by no means often found but a little searching may reveal one for sale. It has of course other uses. It would be ideal as a bedside table, as a small casual table for the sitting room, or in a not-too-large hall, and like some of the other more conventional games tables it could act as a "make do" dining table for one.

Bibliography

Cescinsky, Herbert, *Early English Furniture and Woodwork.*

Cescinsky, Herbert, *English Furniture of the Eighteenth Century.*

Cotterell, Howard H., *Old Pewter.*

Litchfield, Fred, *Pottery and Porcelain.*

Macquoid and Edwards, *Dictionary of English Furniture.*

Masse, H. J. L. J., *The Pewter Collector.*

Percival, MacIver, *The Glass Collector.*

Thorpe, W. A., *English and Irish Glass.*

Veitch, Henry N., *Sheffield Plate.*

Watts, W. W., *Old English Silver.*

Index